RHYMES
OF
REASON

INSPIRATIONAL POEMS TO ENCOURAGE AND ENLIGHTEN

MICHAEL GITTENS

Unless otherwise noted, all Scripture quotations are
taken from the King James Version of the Bible.

Scripture quotations marked (NKJV) are taken from the New King James
Version ®. Copyright © 1982 by Thomas Nelson.
Used by permission. All rights reserved.

Scripture quotations marked (MEV) are taken from the Modern English Version.
Copyright © 2014 by Military Bible Association.
Used by permission. All rights reserved.

Writing style disclosure:
The author's discretion to capitalize certain pronouns that refer to The Lord and
not to capitalize any names related to the devil, is deliberate, though it violates
grammatical rules.

Rhymes of Reason:
Inspirational Poems to encourage and enlighten.
ISBN   978-1-7352277-0-2   paperback
ISBN   978-1-7352277-1-9   hardcover
ISBN   978-1-7352277-2-6   e-book

Copyright © 2020 Michael Gittens

Published by:
Life's Ambition
P,O, Box 2586
Blairsville, GA 30514

Printed in the United States of America.
All rights reserved under International Copyright Law.
Portions of this work may be quoted with proper acknowledgement
limited to the express purpose of the furtherance of The Gospel message
of Jesus Christ and the encouragement and edification of Christendom
TO THE EXCLUSION OF MERCHANDISING FOR PROFIT.
All quotes taken from this work must conform to a verbatim account.
All permission requests for use apart from these specified guidelines
must be approved in writing by the author / publisher.

Credits

Cover Design: Travis A. Dykes
www.travisalan.co

Photo by: Isiah Gibson
www.unsplash.com

Special thanks to Blue Letter Bible, for a wealth of study resources.
www.blueletterbible.org

Dedication

In preparation of our marriage in May of 1984, Marilyn and I sat under the counsel of a wise and capable pastor, a dear friend of the family, who required of us to read a particular book entitled **Love Is Something You Do**.[*] These many wonderful years together, I am blessed beyond measure to have the love of my life still fulfilling the very theme of that book, day by day in countless ways. I have observed her as a caring daughter to both of our parents, a faithful sister, a loving mother, a doting grandmother, a trustworthy friend, a dependable prayer partner, and everything good in my life. I dedicate this book to my partner, my sweetheart, my beautiful wife.
As I thankfully attest to the profound truth of Proverbs 18:22, "He who finds a wife finds a good thing."

---

[*] John R. Bisagno, *Love Is Something You Do* (New York: Harper & Row, 1975).

Acknowledgements

With deep appreciation, I would like to acknowledge those who purposed their lives to knowing God and reflecting His love. Through their relationship with the Lord and dedication to His calling, countless people have been forever changed, inspired, edified and nurtured in the things of God.

I am so grateful to be one of those people "forever changed."

Margarete Woods, my mother, a woman of impeccable character; an ambassador of God's love. Her compassion and giving nature have positively affected so many for time and eternity. She is a shining example of faith in action. Unconditional love and encouragement, blended with structure of ethics, values and determination are just some of the treasures that our mother poured into us. Her commitment bore our opportunities. My brother and I are thankful beyond words for the champion of our hopes and dreams, the faithful advocate of our aspirations, who sacrificed and invested her own life for others...God's precious blessing, our mother.

Theodore & Eliza Woods, my grandparents, "Mamaw & Papaw," two of the finest people I have ever known. In biblical terms, "The salt of the earth." Our family and many others have built lives on the foundation of their example. Hard work, Christian principles, and guiding values; an enduring heritage. The memories of their love & kindness are an inspiration still.

Harold & Miriam Woods, my aunt and uncle, exemplary Christians and benefactors to the Church of God (Cleveland, TN). Integrity and consistency are hallmarks throughout their dedicated career of exceptional achievements. Role models in every arena of life.

Drs. Robert & Ruby Gittens, my aunt and uncle, founding pastors of Revival Tabernacle and multifaceted, multilateral outreach ministries. Distinguished legacy of service is a testament of their lifelong faithfulness to God's calling. (By whom I was set forth and ordained in 2006)

Acknowledgements

Dr. Charles W. Conn; Dr. Ray H. Hughes; Rev. John L. Walker, renowned influential figures in the Church of God (Cleveland, TN). God's anointing and unique gifts on each of their lives made an indelible impact on me. *"History is an indispensable motivation."* mg

Kenneth E. Hagin, known as the "father of the modern faith movement." Nearly seventy years in ministry after God miraculously healed him of an incurable, terminal illness. He and his wife, Oretha, established Kenneth Hagin Ministries, which continues to fulfill God's agenda. *Word of Faith* magazine; Faith Library Publications; Rhema Praise television broadcast, hosted by Rev. Kenneth W. and Lynette Hagin, as they carry on the tradition of excellence in ministry with Rhema Bible Training College and a long list of related associations and international outreaches.

Drs. Rodney & Adonica Howard-Browne, South African born, missionaries to the United States in the 1980s. God's assignment for their life continues to shake the nations of the world. God's manifest love and signs and wonders follow their ministry because of their commitment to follow the Holy Spirit and not the religiosities of man. A ministry characterized by God's mandate of practical application and demonstration of His Word and anointing. Preparing God's people for the final great awakening. Visionaries, leaders, patriotic naturalized American citizens, founding pastors of Revival Ministries International, Inc. (RMI) Their ministry encompasses multiple outreaches, including the River at Tampa Bay Church, the River Bible Institute, River School of Worship and River School of Government. Dedicated to training revivalists for the twenty-first century.

Kenneth & Gloria Copeland, more than fifty-two years in ministry, they share the biblical message of hope and blessing globally from the ministry headquarters in Fort Worth, TX. KCM's purpose is to mature believers worldwide in the use of their faith, centered on the Word of God.

Dr. Bill Winston, founding pastor of Faith Ministries Alliance & Living Word Christian Center, Forest Park, IL.

Acknowledgements

Pastor Keith Moore, founder and president of Faith Life Church, Sarasota, FL, and Branson, MO.

Dr. Myles Monroe, founder of Bahamas Faith Ministries Int. He was a prolific author, pastor, and leader.

Dr. Mark Yarbrough; Dr. James Allman; Dr. Ron Allen; Pres. Dr. Mark Bailey, professors, Dallas Theological Seminary.

Pastor Bob Hoekstra; Pastor Chuck Smith; Pastor David Shirley; Pastor David Hocking, instructors, BLB Institute.

Dr. Dennis Frey, Dr. Gary Fair, Master's International School of Divinity, Evansville, IN

Dr. Bill Mounce, Scholar of New Testament Greek and president of BiblicalTraining.org.

Dr. Bruce Ware, esteemed professor of Theology, BiblicalTraining.org.

Ken Ham, apologist and founder of Answers in Genesis.org

Troy J. Edwards, founder of Vindicating God Ministries and senior pastor of Victorious Word Christian Fellowship Pawtucket, RI.

Sr. Pastor Glenn Lovell, United Christian Faith Ministries, Church Hill, TN. (My ministerial credentialing authority).

The list goes on...

I will forego an attempt to name all the individuals who have shaped my perception and helped me to grow and develop in the things of God, as that is a process and a work that never ends.

May it suffice that I honor the most important of all, the *Holy Spirit Himself*, who has affirmed in me the fundamental scriptural truths that I hold far above compromise or negotiation.

Contents

Credits iii
Dedication v
Acknowledgements vii
Foreword xv
Introduction xvii

Section One: A - E
  Angels Standing By 2
  By Invitation 4
  Choices 6
  Covered 8
  Daily Bread 10
  Earnest of Inheritance 12
  Emmanuel (God with Us) 14
  Exclusive 16
  Extravagant Love 18

Section Two: F - G
  Faith 22
  Foretold Results 24
  Forgiveness 26
  Foundations 28
  Glory to Come 30
  God's Master Plan 32
  God's Righteousness 34
  Grace 38
  Guard Your Heart 40

Section Three: H - L

Higher Laws 44
How Destiny Is Shaped 46
If by Trust 48
Information 50
Integrity.. 52
Jet Airplane 54
Joint Heirs 56
Law of Liberty 58
Legacy 60

Section Four: M - O

Mighty Weapons.. 64
Mode of Operation 66
My Offering 68
My Petition 70
My Portion 72
Never Thirst Again 74
Omniscient 76
Opinions... 78
Order.. 80
Our Sustenance 82

Section Five: P - S

Pentecost 86
Perspective 88
Power of the Tongue 90
Redeemed from the Curse 92
Spiritual Things 94
Standard Weights & Measurements 96
Stop Apostasy 98
Storms 100
Such a Time as This.................................... 102
Sufficient 104

Section Six: T - Z
The Broadcast 108
The Gift 110
The Gospel 112
The Hoax 114
The Premise 116
The Prize 118
The Snake Line 120
Together Once Again 122
Training Wheels 124
Trust the Lord 126
Truth 128
Victory or Defeat 130
What Can't Be Done 132
Your Word 134

Evangelistic Pages
Critical Thinking 137
Personal Note from the Author 141
Understanding Life's Narrative 143
Prayer for Salvation 148
Prayer for the Baptism of the Holy Spirit 150
Notes 155

About the Author 156
Postscript 159

Foreword

I have known Mike for years, a true Christian coworker in the ministry. Reading through the poems he has written in this book, I find the inspiration of Scripture in each one. I believe everyone who reads them should be inspired and empowered to live ever closer to God.

Rev. James A. Hughes, IMNA Founder

The mission of Indian Ministries of North America, Inc. is to be frontline Warriors impacting lives, restoring the broken, healing the wounded, and setting the captives free. We welcome you to our website. You will learn about the vision of IMNA for reaching the Native American people with the gospel of Jesus Christ.

Indianministries.org

Introduction

Thank you for the opportunity to share these poems and thoughts.

It is our highest honor and privilege to participate in things of eternal value. May the body of Christ be edified and the Lord's purpose for this work be *fulfilled* in every way possible (*per 4th bullet point*).

We hope this work will bless you and be an inspiration for teaching others. The following statements provide a brief overview of the message themes and intended objectives in ministering these truths.

- God is perfect Love.
- Love never fails.
- Perfect Love has a perfect will for you... (Plans, Purpose, and Provisions).
- **Perfect Love cannot be fulfilled until it is received.**
- Receiving requires believing.
- Believing is a result of perception.
- Perception is shaped by information.
- Your perception is your reality... Each individual operates within the limits of "their perception." Clearly, not all worldviews/perceptions are based upon truth.
- "Absolute truth exists in and of itself and is not based upon nor subject to man's opinion or intellectual validation." –*mg*

<u>Conclusion:</u>
God's Word is verifiably, the preserved, authoritative, immutable, inerrant, infallible, everlasting and absolute TRUTH.

The most important choice a person can make in life is to seek out, verify, and deposit this absolute truth in their heart.
Thereby, perception allows Perfect Love to be fulfilled.

Section One

A - E

Angels Standing By 2
By Invitation 4
Choices 6
Covered 8
Daily Bread 10
Earnest of Inheritance 12
Emmanuel (God with Us) 14
Exclusive 16
Extravagant Love 18

Angels Standing By

The Lord has given Angels charge
To carry out His will;
Excelling in His Word at large,
Their commission to fulfill.

They minister on our behalf,
By Jesus we are heirs.
How wonderful God's master plan,
Provisions for our care.

In sovereignty God reigns supreme,
Yet honors what we choose;
His plans to be our destiny
Or if we will refuse.

Now set before you, life or death...
All of heaven standing by,
Choices you make will take affect,
Commissioned from on high.

Scriptural Inspiration

Psalm 91:11 For he shall give his angels charge over thee, to keep thee in all thy ways.

Psalm 103:20–21 Bless the LORD, ye his angels, that excel in strength, that do his commandments, hearkening unto the voice of his word. Bless ye the LORD, all ye his hosts; ye ministers of his, that do his pleasure.

Hebrews 1:14 Are they not all ministering spirits, sent forth to minister for them who shall be heirs of salvation?

Romans 8:17 And if children, then heirs; heirs of God, and joint-heirs with Christ; if so be that we suffer with him, that we may be also glorified together.

Jeremiah 29:11 For I know the thoughts that I think toward you, saith the LORD, thoughts of peace, and not of evil, to give you an expected end.

Deuteronomy 30:19 I call heaven and earth to record this day against you, that I have set before you life and death, blessing and cursing: therefore choose life, that both thou and thy seed may live.

By Invitation

With spoken words a thought conveyed
And vision is defined;
As if by artist brush portrayed,
Thus God created life.

Far beyond man's finite mind,
More than we can conceive;
God gave His Word that we may find
Eternal destiny.

His Word reveals and plainly shows,
Perfect plans for our lives.
That all who will may come to know
Perfect love personified.

By invitation we may come
Before the throne of Grace;
Help and mercy there for everyone,
Through Jesus we obtain.

Genesis 1:1 In the beginning God created the heaven and the earth.

Isaiah 55:9 For as the heavens are higher than the earth, so are my ways higher than your ways, and my thoughts than your thoughts.

John 1:1-5, 14 In the beginning was the Word, and the Word was with God, and the Word was God. The same was in the beginning with God. All things were made by him; and without him was not any thing made that was made. In him was life; and the life was the light of men. And the light shineth in darkness; and the darkness comprehended it not. ... And the Word was made flesh, and dwelt among us, (and we beheld his glory, the glory as of the only begotten of the Father,) full of grace and truth.

Matthew 11:28–30 Come unto me, all ye that labor and are heavy laden, and I will give you rest. Take my yoke upon you, and learn of me; for I am meek and lowly in heart: and ye shall find rest unto your souls. For my yoke is easy, and my burden is light.

Hebrews 4:16 Let us therefore come boldly unto the throne of grace, that we may obtain mercy, and find grace to help in time of need.

Choices

So powerful His spoken words,
They're spirit and they're life.
The very premise of this world,
Creation testifies.

Final supreme authority,
By which all things consist.
Yet many people fail to see
The gravity of this.

For God has given man free will,
To choose Him or reject;
Nevertheless, He's sovereign still,
To allow what choice affects.

Be careful that you don't assume
Choice has no consequence;
The Lord will honor what you choose,
Even if you're in contempt.

His perfect will and perfect love
Are constant without change.
But, choice He delegates to us;
So we control our fate.

Scriptural Inspiration

Proverbs 4:20-22 My son, attend to my words; incline thine ear unto my sayings. Let them not depart from thine eyes; keep them in the midst of thine heart. For they are life unto those that find them, and health to all their flesh.

John 6:63 It is the spirit that quickeneth; the flesh profiteth nothing: the words that I speak unto you, they are spirit, and they are life.

Psalm 33:6 By the word of the LORD were the heavens made; and all the host of them by the breath of his mouth.

Colossians 1:17 And he is before all things, and by him all things consist.

Deuteronomy 30:19 I call heaven and earth to record this day against you, that I have set before you life and death, blessing and cursing: therefore choose life, that both thou and thy seed may live.

Jeremiah 29:11 For I know the thoughts that I think toward you, saith the LORD, thoughts of peace, and not of evil, to give you an expected end.

2 Peter 3:9 The Lord is not slack concerning his promise, as some men count slackness; but is longsuffering to us-ward, not willing that any should perish, but that all should come to repentance.

Covered

Remember what our Lord has said,
To watch for His return.
Press on and run the race ahead,
Beyond trials and concerns.

He's mindful of your every step,
He's with you all the way.
There's no need for you to fret,
Just trust Him day by day.

Who was and is and is to come,
By Him all things consist.
Yet He gave Himself a ransom,
To make us His righteousness.

So, in as much as we are clothed
And covered by His Word,
There's nothing this world can withhold
That Jesus has assured.

Scriptural Inspiration

Matthew 24:42 Watch therefore: for ye know not what hour your Lord doth come.

Hebrews 12:1 Wherefore seeing we also are compassed about with so great a cloud of witnesses, let us lay aside every weight, and the sin which doth so easily beset us, and let us run with patience the race that is set before us.

Matthew 6:25-33 Therefore I say unto you, Take no thought for your life, what ye shall eat, or what ye shall drink; nor yet for your body, what ye shall put on. Is not the life more than meat, and the body than raiment? Behold the fowls of the air: for they sow not, neither do they reap, nor gather into barns; yet your heavenly Father feedeth them. Are ye not much better than they? Which of you by taking thought can add one cubit unto his stature? And why take ye thought for raiment? Consider the lilies of the field, how they grow; they toil not, neither do they spin: And yet I say unto you, That even Solomon in all his glory was not arrayed like one of these. Wherefore, if God so clothe the grass of the field, which to day is, and to morrow is cast into the oven, shall he not much more clothe you, O ye of little faith? Therefore take no thought, saying, What shall we eat? or, What shall we drink? or, Wherewithal shall we be clothed? (For after all these things do the Gentiles seek:) for your heavenly Father knoweth that ye have need of all these things. But seek ye first the kingdom of God, and his righteousness; and all these things shall be added unto you.

Revelation 4:8 And the four beasts had each of them six wings about him; and they were full of eyes within: and they rest not day and night, saying, Holy, holy, holy, Lord God Almighty, which was, and is, and is to come.

Colossians 1:17 And he is before all things, and by him all things consist.

1 Timothy 2:6 Who gave himself a ransom for all, to be testified in due time.

2 Corinthians 5:21 For he hath made him to be sin for us, who knew no sin; that we might be made the righteousness of God in him.

Daily Bread

Lord, thank You for Your will for me,
I press on day by day;
And purpose in my heart to be
Committed in that way.

To walk by faith and not by sight;
Your Word can never fail.
I'll run the race and fight the fight;
Your Word makes me prevail.

I refuse a heart of unbelief
That will cause me to come short...
I choose to trust You and receive
The truth of Your report.

I may not know what lies ahead,
The challenges I'll face.
But, You provide my daily bread;
So I shall live by faith.

Philippians 3:14 I press toward the mark for the prize of the high calling of God in Christ Jesus.

2 Corinthians 5:7 (For we walk by faith, not by sight:)

Isaiah 55:11 So shall my word be that goeth forth out of my mouth: it shall not return unto me void, but it shall accomplish that which I please, and it shall prosper in the thing whereto I sent it.

Hebrews 12:1 Wherefore seeing we also are compassed about with so great a cloud of witnesses, let us lay aside every weight, and the sin which doth so easily beset us, and let us run with patience the race that is set before us,

1 Corinthians 9:24 Know ye not that they which run in a race run all, but one receiveth the prize? So run, that ye may obtain.

Hebrews 3:12 Take heed, brethren, lest there be in any of you an evil heart of unbelief, in departing from the living God.

Isaiah 53:1 Who hath believed our report? and to whom is the arm of the LORD revealed?

John 12:38 That the saying of Esaias the prophet might be fulfilled, which he spake, Lord, who hath believed our report? and to whom hath the arm of the Lord been revealed?

Luke 11:3 Give us day by day our daily bread.

Matthew 4:4 But he answered and said, It is written, Man shall not live by bread alone, but by every word that proceedeth out of the mouth of God.

Romans 1:17 For therein is the righteousness of God revealed from faith to faith: as it is written, The just shall live by faith.

Galatians 3:11 But that no man is justified by the law in the sight of God, it is evident: for, The just shall live by faith.

Hebrews 10:38 Now the just shall live by faith: but if any man draw back, my soul shall have no pleasure in him.

Earnest of Inheritance

Treasure in this earthen vessel,
There's nothing to compare.
Every gift unique and special,
In each of us to share.

The finished work of Calvary,
God changed the paradigm,
Of where His temple now will be,
The veil torn as a sign.

Tabernacle of His Glory
Requires protocol.
As in the Holy of Holies,
In Jesus we meet all.

Earnest of our inheritance.
Redemption through His blood.
Lord we are your inhabitance.
Sealed by Your perfect love.

Holy Spirit, in your presence,
We're quickened and endued.
Overwhelmed in reverence,
We bow in awe of you.

Scriptural Inspiration

2 Corinthians 4:7 But we have this treasure in earthen vessels, that the excellency of the power may be of God, and not of us.

1 Corinthians 12:4 Now there are diversities of gifts, but the same Spirit. *(see all of chpt. 12)*

1 Corinthians 6:19 What? know ye not that your body is the temple of the Holy Ghost which is in you, which ye have of God, and ye are not your own?

Mark 15:38 And the veil of the temple was rent in twain from the top to the bottom.

Ephesians 1:14 Which is the earnest of our inheritance until the redemption of the purchased possession, unto the praise of his glory.

Acts 2:39 For the promise is unto you, and to your children, and to all that are afar off, even as many as the Lord our God shall call.

2 Corinthians 1:22 Who hath also sealed us, and given the earnest of the Spirit in our hearts.

Ephesians 1:13 In whom ye also trusted, after that ye heard the word of truth, the gospel of your salvation: in whom also after that ye believed, ye were sealed with that holy Spirit of promise,

Ephesians 4:30 And grieve not the holy Spirit of God, whereby ye are sealed unto the day of redemption.

Luke 24:49 And, behold, I send the promise of my Father upon you: but tarry ye in the city of Jerusalem, until ye be endued with power from on high.

Emmanuel (God with Us)

The everlasting covenant,
God's perfect love and will.
Centered on the great advent
Our Savior did fulfill.

Christ Jesus is our advocate.
God's Word came in the flesh,
Exonerates us from sin debt
We're made His righteousness.

The only one who mediates
Between God and man.
The same who spoke and did create
Time and universe expanse.

He'll never leave us nor forsake,
Our ever present help.
In Him is our eternal fate,
Emmanuel Himself.

Scriptural Inspiration

Genesis 17:7 And I will establish my covenant between me and thee and thy seed after thee in their generations for an everlasting covenant, to be a God unto thee, and to thy seed after thee.

Isaiah 9:6 For unto us a child is born, unto us a son is given: and the government shall be upon his shoulder: and his name shall be called Wonderful, Counsellor, The mighty God, The everlasting Father, The Prince of Peace.

1 John 2:1 My little children, these things write I unto you, that ye sin not. And if any man sin, we have an advocate with the Father, Jesus Christ the righteous:

John 1:14 And the Word was made flesh, and dwelt among us, (and we beheld his glory, the glory as of the only begotten of the Father,) full of grace and truth.

2 Corinthians 5:21 For he hath made him to be sin for us who knew no sin; that we might be made the righteousness of God in him.

1 Timothy 2:5 For there is one God, and one mediator between God and men, the man Christ Jesus;

Colossians 1:16 For by him were all things created, that are in heaven, and that are in earth, visible and invisible, whether they be thrones, or dominions, or principalities, or powers: all things were created by him, and for him:

Hebrews 13:5 Let your conversation be without covetousness; and be content with such things as ye have: for he hath said, I will never leave thee, nor forsake thee.

Psalm 46:1 God is our refuge and strength, a very present help in trouble.

Matthew 1:23 Behold, a virgin shall be with child, and shall bring forth a son, and they shall call his name Emmanuel, which being interpreted is, God with us.

Exclusive

In Christendom it's sad to see
Apostasy creep in;
The very Word some won't believe
Is where faith must begin!

Faith centered on God's Word alone,
Not conjecture or debate;
We have His Word, He's made it known,
Why do they speculate?

Preserved, inerrant, absolute,
God's Word will never change.
Infallible eternal truth
Resides in Jesus' name.

Salvation comes no other way,
Exclusively God's plan.
It matters not what people say,
Only God, the Great I Am.

Scriptural Inspiration

Galatians 3:22 But the scripture hath concluded all under sin, that the promise by faith of Jesus Christ might be given to them that believe.

2 Timothy 3:16 All scripture is given by inspiration of God, and is profitable for doctrine, for reproof, for correction, for instruction in righteousness:

Psalm 89:34 My covenant will I not break, nor alter the thing that is gone out of my lips.

Psalm 119:89 For ever, O LORD, thy word is settled in heaven.

Matthew 28:18 And Jesus came and spake unto them, saying, All power is given unto me in heaven and in earth.

Acts 4:12 Neither is there salvation in any other: for there is none other name under heaven given among men, whereby we must be saved.

Ephesians 1:21 Far above all principality, and power, and might, and dominion, and every name that is named, not only in this world, but also in that which is to come:

Philippians 2:9 Wherefore God also hath highly exalted him, and given him a name which is above every name:

John 14:6 Jesus saith unto him, I am the way, the truth, and the life: no man cometh unto the Father, but by me.

Extravagant Love

I walk this path but not alone,
For Jesus does abide.
He lets me know I am His own,
He's with me day and night.

I thank You, Lord, for perfect love,
That washes over me.
Your Word is more than just enough,
Extravagant love decreed !

He keeps those in perfect peace,
Whose mind is stayed on Him.
And He supplies our every need,
Free from the bonds of sin.

The essence, Lord, of who You are,
Is Your anointed Word;
There You reveal to us Your heart
Your perfect love assured.

Deuteronomy 31:6 Be strong and of a good courage, fear not, nor be afraid of them: for the LORD thy God, he it is that doth go with thee; he will not fail thee, nor forsake thee.

Matthew 4:4 But he answered and said, It is written, Man shall not live by bread alone, but by every word that proceedeth out of the mouth of God.

2 Peter 1:4 Whereby are given unto us exceeding great and precious promises: that by these ye might be partakers of the divine nature, having escaped the corruption that is in the world through lust.

Isaiah 26:3 Thou wilt keep him in perfect peace, whose mind is stayed on thee: because he trusteth in thee.

Philippians 4:19 But my God shall supply all your need according to his riches in glory by Christ Jesus.

Isaiah 10:27 And it shall come to pass in that day, that his burden shall be taken away from off thy shoulder, and his yoke from off thy neck, and the yoke shall be destroyed because of the anointing.

John 1:1 In the beginning was the Word, and the Word was with God, and the Word was God.

Section Two

F - G

Faith	22
Foretold Results	24
Forgiveness	26
Foundations	28
Glory to Come	30
God's Master Plan	32
God's Righteousness	34
Grace	38
Guard Your Heart	40

Faith

Having done all to stand,
Confessed God's Word, and prayed,
Yet the challenge still at hand
And victory seems delayed.

You must know and not forget
His Word can never fail.
Have patience and avoid regret,
Perseverance will prevail.

Take heart for you are not alone,
Many have gone before.
Their faith to us examples shown
As Scripture does implore.

Set aside every weight and sin
That does so easily beset.
Remember that the race you're in
Requires faith for every step.

Ephesians 6:11-18 Put on the whole armour of God, that ye may be able to stand against the wiles of the devil. For we wrestle not against flesh and blood, but against principalities, against powers, against the rulers of the darkness of this world, against spiritual wickedness in high places. Wherefore take unto you the whole armour of God, that ye may be able to withstand in the evil day, and having done all, to stand. Stand therefore, having your loins girt about with truth, and having on the breastplate of righteousness; And your feet shod with the preparation of the gospel of peace; Above all, taking the shield of faith, wherewith ye shall be able to quench all the fiery darts of the wicked. And take the helmet of salvation, and the sword of the Spirit, which is the word of God: Praying always with all prayer and supplication in the Spirit, and watching thereunto with all perseverance and supplication for all saints;

(See all of James chpt. 1)

Hebrews 10:35-39 Cast not away therefore your confidence, which hath great recompence of reward. For ye have need of patience, that, after ye have done the will of God, ye might receive the promise. For yet a little while, and he that shall come will come, and will not tarry. Now the just shall live by faith: but if any man draw back, my soul shall have no pleasure in him. But we are not of them who draw back unto perdition; but of them that believe to the saving of the soul.

Hebrews 11:1 Now faith is the substance of things hoped for, the evidence of things not seen.

(See all of Hebrews chpt. 11)

Hebrews 12:1,2 Wherefore seeing we also are compassed about with so great a cloud of witnesses, let us lay aside every weight, and the sin which doth so easily beset us, and let us run with patience the race that is set before us, Looking unto Jesus the author and finisher of our faith; who for the joy that was set before him endured the cross, despising the shame, and is set down at the right hand of the throne of God.

Foretold Results

Faith principles must operate
For manifest results.
Cause and effect always dictate
The narrative for us.

Creation's order in all things,
The Lord's perfect design;
Compliance with these laws will bring
Foretold results each time.

Desired results require action,
They're not by accident;
Press in to learn what must be done,
Your time will be well spent.

Due diligence has great reward,
It's not mysterious!
Two plus two is always four,
It works for all of us.

Scriptural Inspiration

Hebrews 11:6 But without faith it is impossible to please him: for he that cometh to God must believe that he is, and that he is a rewarder of them that diligently seek him.

Exposition:
"Compliance to order is essential for success in any objective."
The laws and principles which govern all of creation are easy to recognize. These foundational laws and principles are constant and fixed in the intricate design and function of all that God created. Many brilliant minds have dedicated their lives to understanding the depth and implications of those laws and principles, as they apply to various disciplines of science. Throughout history, humankind has advanced in knowledge, skills and ability, in every arena of life. A practical application of known laws and principles have produced desired results and quality of life in the human experience. In everything from the invention of the wheel, to heart transplants; From jet airplanes, to wireless communications... Yet, not one technological advancement, not one scientific advancement ever came to fruition apart from the inherent operation of the laws and principles associated with that respective discipline. As far as we have come since the garden of Eden, the most brilliant minds are still seeking to understand the inexhaustible detail of order that presides over God's creation.

The point of focus here is that order is the premise of how **everything** works. Recognizing that order, and operating within the laws and principles of order is the only way to actuate or produce desired results.

The premise of order by which laws and principles determine the outcome of everything in the natural realm, is the very same premise by which everything operates in the spiritual realm. A practical application of the laws and principals of God's Word, (The Bible), will produce the intended desired results. All by God's design, for our benefit. Just read **Isaiah chapter 55** to learn how God's Word accomplishes what He sent it to do.

God's Word is the essence of God Himself; Perfect Love personified. His Word is His explicit perfect will and plans for you.

Do you find these thoughts compelling? Do you feel a hunger and a desire to pursue God's plans and purpose? If your answer is yes, I believe this is more than a chance encounter that you are reading this little book.

"God Bless You." - *MG*

Forgiveness

Just as sure as we're forgiven,
Our mandate is the same.
Reciprocate the grace we live in,
By choices that we make.

Bitterness and unforgiveness
Are toxic, they destroy!
Never let them live within us,
Commanded by the Lord.

Perfect love, God's disposition,
His essence is our gift.
Eternal life through Jesus given
Reflects His love, to wit.

Forgive just as we're forgiven,
As we are saved by grace.
If we're to have this grace provision,
Then, we must do the same.

1 John 1:9 If we confess our sins, he is faithful and just to forgive us our sins, and to cleanse us from all unrighteousness.

Mark 11:25-26 And when ye stand praying, forgive, if ye have ought against any: that your Father also which is in heaven may forgive you your trespasses. But if ye do not forgive, neither will your Father which is in heaven forgive your trespasses.

Hebrews 12:15 Looking diligently lest any man fail of the grace of God; lest any root of bitterness springing up trouble you, and thereby many be defiled;

Romans 5:8 But God commendeth his love toward us, in that, while we were yet sinners, Christ died for us.

Matthew 6:12 And forgive us our debts, as we forgive our debtors.

Luke 4:4 And Jesus answered him, saying, It is written, That man shall not live by bread alone, but by every word of God.

Foundations

The temporal is subordinate
To the eternal realm.
We do well to not forget
This premise at the helm.

For all that's seen will pass away;
Sin's entropic effects.
Yet unseen things will never fade,
God told us to expect.

The essence of the power by which
Creation came to be;
He called forth out of nothingness
Everything that can be seen.

The natural realm thereby sustained
By that which is unseen;
Foundations that will never change,
God set forth as supreme.

So learn these laws and principles,
In all things they apply;
His Word affects the temporal
If in Jesus we abide.

Scriptural Inspiration

2 Corinthians 4:18 (MEV) while we do not look at the things which are seen, but at the things which are not seen. For the things which are seen are temporal, but the things which are not seen are eternal.

Hebrews 11:3 (MEV) By faith we understand that the universe was framed by the word of God, so that things that are seen were not made out of things which are visible.

Mark 11:20-26 (MEV) In the morning, as they passed by, they saw the fig tree withered from the roots. Peter, calling to remembrance, said to Him, "Rabbi, look! The fig tree which You cursed has withered away." Jesus answered them, "Have faith in God. For truly I say to you, whoever says to this mountain, 'Be removed and be thrown into the sea,' and does not doubt in his heart, but believes that what he says will come to pass, he will have whatever he says. Therefore I say to you, whatever things you ask when you pray, believe that you will receive them, and you will have them. And when you stand praying, forgive if you have anything against anyone, so that your Father who is in heaven may also forgive you your sins. But if you do not forgive, neither will your Father who is in heaven forgive your sins."

John 15:4-7 Abide in me, and I in you. As the branch cannot bear fruit of itself, except it abide in the vine; no more can ye, except ye abide in me. I am the vine, ye are the branches: He that abideth in me, and I in him, the same bringeth forth much fruit: for without me ye can do nothing. If a man abide not in me, he is cast forth as a branch, and is withered; and men gather them, and cast them into the fire, and they are burned. If ye abide in me, and my words abide in you, ye shall ask what ye will, and it shall be done unto you.

Glory to Come

For now we only dimly see,
As through glass obscure.
But when we reach eternity,
Perfect clarity assured.

For what we see is temporal,
Bound to pass away.
But things to come forevermore,
Perfect Love gives perfect fate.

Hold fast to all that cannot fail,
The plans of perfect Love.
By simply trusting we avail,
To all God made for us.

These light afflictions can't compare,
With Glory that's to come.
The Lord's provision is our share,
Perfect Love has only just begun.

Scriptural Inspiration

1 Corinthians 13:12 For now we see through a glass, darkly; but then face to face: now I know in part; but then shall I know even as also I am known.

2 Corinthians 4:18 While we look not at the things which are seen, but at the things which are not seen: for the things which are seen are temporal; but the things which are not seen are eternal.

Hebrews 10:23 Let us hold fast the profession of our faith without wavering; (for he is faithful that promised;)

Hebrews 10:35-38 Cast not away therefore your confidence, which hath great recompence of reward. or ye have need of patience, that, after ye have done the will of God, ye might receive the promise. For yet a little while, and he that shall come will come, and will not tarry. Now the just shall live by faith: but if any man draw back, my soul shall have no pleasure in him.

Mat 6:33 But seek ye first the kingdom of God, and his righteousness; and all these things shall be added unto you.

2 Corinthians 4:17 For our light affliction, which is but for a moment, worketh for us a far more exceeding and eternal weight of glory;

God's Master Plan

As ambassadors we represent
God's kingdom that presides.
His master plan and His intent
For earth and all mankind.

For everyone who will repent
And be redeemed from sin,
Through Jesus whom the Father sent
To restore mankind to Him.

The story of that great event
That happened as God planned,
Fulfilled His Word and covenant
He made with Abraham.

He was wounded for our transgressions,
Bruised for our iniquities.
The High Priest of our confession,
Jesus came to set us free.

He bore our grief and sorrows
And suffered for our peace.
From sin's penalty He pardoned
And by His stripes we're healed.

Scriptural Inspiration

Ephesians 6:19-20 And for me, that utterance may be given unto me, that I may open my mouth boldly, to make known the mystery of the gospel, For which I am an ambassador in bonds: that therein I may speak boldly, as I ought to speak.

John 3:16-17 For God so loved the world, that he gave his only begotten Son, that whosoever believeth in him should not perish, but have everlasting life. For God sent not his Son into the world to condemn the world; but that the world through him might be saved.

1 John 4:9 In this was manifested the love of God toward us, because that God sent his only begotten Son into the world, that we might live through him.

Genesis 17:7 And I will establish my covenant between me and thee and thy seed after thee in their generations for an everlasting covenant, to be a God unto thee, and to thy seed after thee.

Psalm 105:8-10 He hath remembered his covenant for ever, the word which he commanded to a thousand generations. Which covenant he made with Abraham, and his oath unto Isaac; And confirmed the same unto Jacob for a law, and to Israel for an everlasting covenant:

Isaiah 53:5 But he was wounded for our transgressions, he was bruised for our iniquities: the chastisement of our peace was upon him; and with his stripes we are healed. (Also see: **1 Peter 2:24** and **Matthew 8:17**)

Hebrews 3:1 Wherefore, holy brethren, partakers of the heavenly calling, consider the Apostle and High Priest of our profession, Christ Jesus;

Hebrews 4:14-16 Seeing then that we have a great high priest, that is passed into the heavens, Jesus the Son of God, let us hold fast our profession. For we have not an high priest which cannot be touched with the feeling of our infirmities; but was in all points tempted like as we are, yet without sin. Let us therefore come boldly unto the throne of grace, that we may obtain mercy, and find grace to help in time of need.

God's Righteousness

We have been made God's righteousness
By Jesus Christ our Lord;
Conferred upon us meritless,
We can't earn what He affords.

By perfect love we're justified,
Just-as-if-I'd never sinned.
The covenant Jesus ratified
By which we're born again.

He gave Himself to set us free
From consequence of sin;
If His salvation you receive
And give yourself to Him.

Make Him your Lord, preeminent,
Let Him direct your life,
That He may give His providence
And you can be a light.

Will you be an ambassador
And represent God's love ?
Teach people to make Jesus Lord,
Their works aren't good enough.

2 Corinthians 5:21 For he hath made him to be sin for us, who knew no sin; that we might be made the righteousness of God in him.

Titus 3:5 Not by works of righteousness which we have done, but according to his mercy he saved us, by the washing of regeneration, and renewing of the Holy Ghost;

Ephesians 2:9 Not of works, lest any man should boast.

Galatians 2:16 Knowing that a man is not justified by the works of the law, but by the faith of Jesus Christ, even we have believed in Jesus Christ, that we might be justified by the faith of Christ, and not by the works of the law: for by the works of the law shall no flesh be justified.

1 Timothy 2:6 Who gave himself a ransom for all, to be testified in due time.

Galatians 3:13-14 Christ hath redeemed us from the curse of the law, being made a curse for us: for it is written, Cursed is every one that hangeth on a tree: That the blessing of Abraham might come on the Gentiles through Jesus Christ; that we might receive the promise of the Spirit through faith.

Romans 8:14 For as many as are led by the Spirit of God, they are the sons of God.

Ephesians 5:8 For ye were sometimes darkness, but now are ye light in the Lord: walk as children of light:

Galatians 2:16 Knowing that a man is not justified by the works of the law, but by the faith of Jesus Christ, even we have believed in Jesus Christ, that we might be justified by the faith of Christ, and not by the works of the law: for by the works of the law shall no flesh be justified.

Ephesians 2:8-9 For by grace are ye saved through faith; and that not of yourselves: it is the gift of God: Not of works, lest any man should boast.

God's Words Are Life

We must walk by faith, not by sight,
God's Word is all we need.
For not by power nor by might,
But by His Spirit we succeed.

Your Word forever settled, Lord,
From beginning to the end.
You watch over to perform
All of Your promises, Amen.

Your Perfect Love gives perfect peace,
To whose mind is stayed on You.
 Love that cannot fail or cease,
Your Word forever true.

Your words are life to those who find,
And health to all their flesh.
We purpose in our heart and mind,
To enter in Your rest.

2 Corinthians 5:7 (For we walk by faith, not by sight:)

Zechariah 4:6 Then he answered and spake unto me, saying, This is the word of the LORD unto Zerubbabel, saying, Not by might, nor by power, but by my spirit, saith the LORD of hosts.

Psalm 119:89 For ever, O LORD, thy word is settled in heaven.

Luke 21:33 Heaven and earth shall pass away: but my words shall not pass away.

Jeremiah 1:12 Then said the LORD unto me, Thou hast well seen: for I will hasten my word to perform it.

2 Corinthians 1:20 For all the promises of God in him are yea, and in him Amen, unto the glory of God by us.

Isaiah 26:3 Thou wilt keep him in perfect peace, whose mind is stayed on thee: because he trusteth in thee.

Proverbs 4:20-22 My son, attend to my words; incline thine ear unto my sayings. Let them not depart from thine eyes; keep them in the midst of thine heart. For they are life unto those that find them, and health to all their flesh.

Hebrews 4:9-11 There remaineth therefore a rest to the people of God. For he that is entered into his rest, he also hath ceased from his own works, as God did from his. Let us labour therefore to enter into that rest, lest any man fall after the same example of unbelief.

Grace

The Grace of God forever free,
It comes by perfect Love.
Conditioned on if we believe
This gift from God above.

For with the heart we do receive
The righteousness He gives.
Jesus came and made me free,
And in Him now I live.

Confession is what brings to bear
The plans of perfect Love,
For in Him you shall have no care
If only you will trust.

Scriptural Inspiration

Romans 6:23 For the wages of sin is death; but the gift of God is eternal life through Jesus Christ our Lord.

Romans 10:10 For with the heart man believeth unto righteousness; and with the mouth confession is made unto salvation.

1 Peter 5:7 Casting all your care upon him; for he careth for you.

Guard Your Heart

What you give place to and allow
Becomes what you desire.
There's no mystery about how
Small kindling starts the fire.

That's why God warns to guard your heart,
Thereby control your life.
Destiny by choice your part,
Rewards for every fight.

The enemy has come to lie,
Steal, kill, and destroy.
But with Jesus ever by your side,
The victory is yours.

Submit yourself to God each day,
Resist evil and it flees.
The Word of God will make your way,
Sustains your every need.

Scriptural Inspiration

James 3:5-6 Even so the tongue is a little member, and boasteth great things. Behold, how great a matter a little fire kindleth! And the tongue is a fire, a world of iniquity: so is the tongue among our members, that it defileth the whole body, and setteth on fire the course of nature; and it is set on fire of hell.

Proverbs 4:23 Keep thy heart with all diligence; for out of it are the issues of life.

(See all of Ephesians chpt.. 4)

John 10:10 The thief cometh not, but for to steal, and to kill, and to destroy: I am come that they might have life, and that they might have it more abundantly.

James 4:7 Submit yourselves therefore to God. Resist the devil, and he will flee from you.

Section Three

H - L

Higher Laws	44
How Destiny Is Shaped	46
If by Trust	48
Information	50
Integrity	52
Jet Airplane	54
Joint Heirs	56
Law of Liberty	58
Legacy	60

Higher Laws

Operating in the higher realm,
Spiritual laws dictate.
Where nature's order is the norm
Results excellerate.

Great power in the spoken word,
God gave us this mandate;
Speak to the mountains and observe
How destiny is shaped.

To actuate those higher laws
How much faith does it take?
A mustard seed is very small,
Jesus used to illustrate.

Perception, the important key
To having what you say;
God's Word must be what you believe
And practice everyday.

Oh, by the way, please be advised,
Confession works both ways.
God's Word opposed or compromised
Results follow the same.

Mark 11:23-24 For verily I say unto you, That whosoever shall say unto this mountain, Be thou removed, and be thou cast into the sea; and shall not doubt in his heart, but shall believe that those things which he saith shall come to pass; he shall have whatsoever he saith. Therefore I say unto you, What things soever ye desire, when ye pray, believe that ye receive them, and ye shall have them.

Matthew 17:20 And Jesus said unto them, Because of your unbelief: for verily I say unto you, If ye have faith as a grain of mustard seed, ye shall say unto this mountain, Remove hence to yonder place; and it shall remove; and nothing shall be impossible unto you.

Mark 9:23 Jesus said unto him, If thou canst believe, all things are possible to him that believeth.

Luke 6:45 A good man out of the good treasure of his heart bringeth forth that which is good; and an evil man out of the evil treasure of his heart bringeth forth that which is evil: for of the abundance of the heart his mouth speaketh.

Matthew 12:37 For by thy words thou shalt be justified, and by thy words thou shalt be condemned.

How Destiny Is Shaped

In God's Word He describes Himself,
His character, and will.
Trust what He says and nothing else,
He's faithful to fulfill.

Solutions there for all to find,
No matter what the need.
The Word of God for all mankind,
Throughout eternity.

Unchanging and forever true,
From God, the Great I Am.
For in Him we all live and move,
And all we need we have.

Provisions come by Perfect Love,
Impossible to fail.
Exceeding far beyond enough,
His Word makes us prevail.

The choice is yours what you believe,
Thereby control your fate;
For as you choose you will receive,
And destiny is shaped.

Scriptural Inspiration

Proverbs 4:20-22 My son, attend to my words; incline thine ear unto my sayings. Let them not depart from thine eyes; keep them in the midst of thine heart. For they are life unto those that find them, and health to all their flesh.

Psalm 119:89 For ever, O LORD, thy word is settled in heaven.

Psalm 89:34 My covenant will I not break, nor alter the thing that is gone out of my lips.

Acts 17:28 For in him we live, and move, and have our being; as certain also of your own poets have said, For we are also his offspring.

Philippians 4:19 But my God shall supply all your need according to his riches in glory by Christ Jesus.

Ephesians 3:20 Now unto him that is able to do exceeding abundantly above all that we ask or think, according to the power that worketh in us,

Romans 10:9 That if thou shalt confess with thy mouth the Lord Jesus, and shalt believe in thine heart that God hath raised him from the dead, thou shalt be saved.

If by Trust

If by trust this fate I gain,
To see His will fulfilled.
Then I must press through any pain,
Beyond limits of my skill.

Through Christ I can do all things,
He strengthens me each day.
No matter what tomorrow brings,
The just shall live by faith.

Put on the armor God provides,
Take sword and shield of faith.
And as the pen of a writer,
My tongue declares God's way.

It is not by might or by power,
But by Christ I overcome,
Every snare set by the fowler,
'Til my journey here is done.

Philippians 4:13 I can do all things through Christ which strengtheneth me.

Romans 1:17 For therein is the righteousness of God revealed from faith to faith: as it is written, The just shall live by faith.

Galatians 3:11 But that no man is justified by the law in the sight of God, it is evident: for, The just shall live by faith.

Hebrews 10:38 Now the just shall live by faith: but if any man draw back, my soul shall have no pleasure in him.

Ephesians 6:11-13 Put on the whole armour of God, that ye may be able to stand against the wiles of the devil. For we wrestle not against flesh and blood, but against principalities, against powers, against the rulers of the darkness of this world, against spiritual wickedness in high places. Wherefore take unto you the whole armour of God, that ye may be able to withstand in the evil day, and having done all, to stand. Stand therefore...(see 14-18)

Psalm 45:1 My heart is inditing a good matter: I speak of the things which I have made touching the king: my tongue is the pen of a ready writer.

Zechariah 4:6 Then he answered and spake unto me, saying, This is the word of the LORD unto Zerubbabel, saying, Not by might, nor by power, but by my spirit, saith the LORD of hosts.

Psalm 91:3 Surely he shall deliver thee from the snare of the fowler, and from the noisome pestilence.

Information

Beyond the limits of our sight,
Beyond the clear blue sky.
Beyond the stars we see at night,
Much more than meets the eye.

Like beautiful horizons flee,
Based on where we stand.
Merely the distance we can see,
Oh, the limits of a man.

Almighty God is not confined
To what we may perceive.
The limits of our finite minds;
What has shaped what you believe?

Information shapes our worldview,
Perceptions then take hold.
Seek the truth that's absolute
Allow God's plans to unfold.

Romans 12:1-2 I beseech you therefore, brethren, by the mercies of God, that ye present your bodies a living sacrifice, holy, acceptable unto God, which is your reasonable service. And be not conformed to this world: but be ye transformed by the renewing of your mind, that ye may prove what is that good, and acceptable, and perfect, will of God.

2 Corinthians 10:4-5 (For the weapons of our warfare are not carnal, but mighty through God to the pulling down of strongholds;) Casting down imaginations, and every high thing that exalteth itself against the knowledge of God, and bringing into captivity every thought to the obedience of Christ;

Integrity

If any two agree on earth
As touching any thing,
Our Lord has given us His Word
The answer He will bring.

He's not a man that He can lie,
His Word can never fail;
Forever settled and defined,
His perfect love and will.

Integrity is the hallmark,
What God says, He will do.
Believing is the only part
Required of me and you.

Be careful that you don't come short
Of promises He made;
By unbelief you will abort
His plans to make your way.

Scriptural Inspiration

Matthew 18:19 Again I say unto you, That if two of you shall agree on earth as touching any thing that they shall ask, it shall be done for them of my Father which is in heaven.

Numbers 23:19 God is not a man, that he should lie; neither the son of man, that he should repent: hath he said, and shall he not do it? or hath he spoken, and shall he not make it good?

Psalm 119:89 For ever, O LORD, thy word is settled in heaven.

Mark 9:23 Jesus said unto him, If thou canst believe, all things are possible to him that believeth.

Hebrews 4:1 Let us therefore fear, lest, a promise being left us of entering into his rest, any of you should seem to come short of it.

Jet Airplane

Developed exponentially,
Mankind has come so far;
In knowledge and technologies,
To get to where we are.

It's taken us six thousand years,
We've only just begun
To understand a little here
Of what's existed since week one.

God's account of His creation,
Six days and He was done;
And just for our information,
"Nothing new under the sun."

A jet airplane could have flown,
Over the Eden garden!
It took some time to come to know,
Physics God imparted.

Scriptural Inspiration

Genesis 1:1 In the beginning God created the heaven and the earth.

Genesis 1:31 And God saw every thing that he had made, and, behold, it was very good. And the evening and the morning were the sixth day.

Genesis 2:1-2 Thus the heavens and the earth were finished, and all the host of them. And on the seventh day God ended his work which he had made; and he rested on the seventh day from all his work which he had made.

Ecclesiastes 1:9 The thing that hath been, it is that which shall be; and that which is done is that which shall be done: and there is no new thing under the sun.

Joint Heirs

Mephibosheth was King Saul's grandson,
He lived in Lo Debar.
Of Saul's bloodline, the last one.
Yet lived beneath his part.

King David called Mephibosheth,
"Come take your rightful place;
In my house the table's set,
I've made for you a space."

Mephibosheth's low self-esteem
Had caused him to despair;
Crippled with no hope, it seemed,
Though he was a royal heir.

Like Christians that have been deceived,
They've bought into the lies;
Not understanding what it means,
"Joint heirs with Jesus Christ."

2 Samuel 9:6-7 Now when Mephibosheth, the son of Jonathan, the son of Saul, was come unto David, he fell on his face, and did reverence. And David said, Mephibosheth. And he answered, Behold thy servant! And David said unto him, Fear not: for I will surely shew thee kindness for Jonathan thy father's sake, and will restore thee all the land of Saul thy father; and thou shalt eat bread at my table continually. **(See all of chpt. 9)**

Romans 8:17 And if children, then heirs; heirs of God, and joint-heirs with Christ; if so be that we suffer with him, that we may be also glorified together. **(See all of chpt. 8)**

Galatians 3:29 And if ye be Christ's, then are ye Abraham's seed, and heirs according to the promise. **(See all of chpt. 3)**

Law of Liberty

God's perfect law of liberty,
James one verse twenty five.
Instruction how to be set free
From bondage in this life.

It's not enough to only hear
God's plan for our success.
But in our doing, it is clear
We have His plans to bless.

When actions correspond with faith
Results always ensue.
For by design this is God's way,
His plans fulfilled in you.

This perfect law is not by chance,
You must choose to comply.
The plans of perfect love advance,
  As you do... and testify.

Scriptural Inspiration

James 1:22-25 But be ye doers of the word, and not hearers only, deceiving your own selves. For if any be a hearer of the word, and not a doer, he is like unto a man beholding his natural face in a glass: For he beholdeth himself, and goeth his way, and straightway forgetteth what manner of man he was. But whoso looketh into the perfect law of liberty, and continueth therein, he being not a forgetful hearer, but a doer of the work, this man shall be blessed in his deed.

Hebrews 11:1 Now faith is the substance of things hoped for, the evidence of things not seen. **(see all of chpt. 11)**

Hebrews 11:6 But without faith it is impossible to please him: for he that cometh to God must believe that he is, and that he is a rewarder of them that diligently seek him.

Deuteronomy 30:19 I call heaven and earth to record this day against you, that I have set before you life and death, blessing and cursing: therefore choose life, that both thou and thy seed may live:

Legacy

A life that's lived with no regrets,
For which we all should strive;
When legacy that will be left,
Reflects a well lived life.

Time doesn't wait for anyone,
So quickly seems to pass.
Who have I helped, what have I done,
In acts of love that last?

Eternity is not too far.
Soon a day will come,
From all we know we will depart,
When life on earth is done.

The eye has never seen before,
Nor known by heart of man,
The things that our God has in store,
Perfect love fulfilled, Amen.

1 Corinthians 13:1 Though I speak with the tongues of men and of angels, and have not charity, I am become as sounding brass, or a tinkling cymbal.

1 Corinthians 2:9 But as it is written, Eye hath not seen, nor ear heard, neither have entered into the heart of man, the things which God hath prepared for them that love him.

Section Four

M - O

Mighty Weapons 64
Mode of Operation 66
My Offering 68
My Petition 70
My Portion 72
Never Thirst Again 74
Omniscient 76
Opinions 78
Order 80
Our Sustenance 82

Mighty Weapons

For everything opposing truth
There is a certain fate.
God's Word and ways are absolute
And not up for debate.

The enemy would have you think
That truth is relative;
he knows this leads to your defeat,
he's cunningly deceptive.

Like postmodernism worldview,
Violates the laws of logic;
Designed to undermine God's plans for you
Unless you recognize it.

The weaponry of our defense
Is mighty through the Lord.
Bring thoughts into obedience
Judged by the Lord's report.

Hallelujah!
"I am more than a conqueror through Christ."

Hebrews 10:26-27 For if we sin wilfully after that we have received the knowledge of the truth, there remaineth no more sacrifice for sins, But a certain fearful looking for of judgment and fiery indignation, which shall devour the adversaries.

1 Corinthians 2:9-14 But as it is written, Eye hath not seen, nor ear heard, neither have entered into the heart of man, the things which God hath prepared for them that love him. But God hath revealed them unto us by his Spirit: for the Spirit searcheth all things, yea, the deep things of God. For what man knoweth the things of a man, save the spirit of man which is in him? even so the things of God knoweth no man, but the Spirit of God. Now we have received, not the spirit of the world, but the spirit which is of God; that we might know the things that are freely given to us of God. Which things also we speak, not in the words which man's wisdom teacheth, but which the Holy Ghost teacheth; comparing spiritual things with spiritual. But the natural man receiveth not the things of the Spirit of God: for they are foolishness unto him: neither can he know them, because they are spiritually discerned.

2 Corinthians 10:4-5 (For the weapons of our warfare are not carnal, but mighty through God to the pulling down of strong holds;) Casting down imaginations, and every high thing that exalteth itself against the knowledge of God, and bringing into captivity every thought to the obedience of Christ;

Mode of Operation

Notice the laws and principles
That govern all that is,
Order does preside in all
To each expected end.

By the spoken Word of God,
Creation came to be.
He called forth things that were not,
Of realms unseen and seen.

By this same modus operandi
He calls us to transcend.
For by our words we're justified,
Or by our words condemned.

Our tongue sets the course direction,
Like the rudder of a ship.
So be careful your confession,
Words shape the life you live.

"We use words to express what we believe…
We set the course of our destiny by the words we speak." –mg

Ecclesiastes 3:1 To every thing there is a season, and a time to every purpose under the heaven. **(See all of chpt. 3)**

Genesis 1:1 In the beginning God created the heaven and the earth. **(See all of chpt. 1)**

Hebrews 11:3 Through faith we understand that the worlds were framed by the word of God, so that things which are seen were not made of things which do appear.

Mark 11:23 For verily I say unto you, That whosoever shall say unto this mountain, Be thou removed, and be thou cast into the sea; and shall not doubt in his heart, but shall believe that those things which he saith shall come to pass; he shall have whatsoever he saith.

Matthew 12:36-37 But I say unto you, That every idle word that men shall speak, they shall give account thereof in the day of judgment. For by thy words thou shalt be justified, and by thy words thou shalt be condemned.

James 3:2-5 For in many things we offend all. If any man offend not in word, the same is a perfect man, and able also to bridle the whole body. Behold, we put bits in the horses' mouths, that they may obey us; and we turn about their whole body. Behold also the ships, which though they be so great, and are driven of fierce winds, yet are they turned about with a very small helm, whithersoever the governor listeth. Even so the tongue is a little member, and boasteth great things. Behold, how great a matter a little fire kindleth!

Matthew 15:18 But those things which proceed out of the mouth come forth from the heart; and they defile the man.

My Offering

Preeminent Majestic King,
By whom we do exist;
I come before You, Lord, to bring
This offering, my gift.

Made worthy by Your Perfect Love,
Acceptable to give.
It's only by your Grace, enough,
An offering like this.

The only thing that I can bring.
For, Lord, it's all I have.
So, thank You for receiving me,
The gift of all I am.

Forever as I live and breathe,
Lord, I belong to You.
Please fulfill all Your plans in me
And all You want to do.

1 Chronicles 29:11 Thine, O LORD, is the greatness, and the power, and the glory, and the victory, and the majesty: for all that is in the heaven and in the earth is thine; thine is the kingdom, O LORD, and thou art exalted as head above all.

Acts 17:28 For in him we live, and move, and have our being; as certain also of your own poets have said, For we are also his offspring.

Romans 3:24 Being justified freely by his grace through the redemption that is in Christ Jesus.

Romans 12:1 I beseech you therefore, brethren, by the mercies of God, that ye present your bodies a living sacrifice, holy, acceptable unto God, which is your reasonable service.

1 Corinthians 6:19-20 What? know ye not that your body is the temple of the Holy Ghost which is in you, which ye have of God, and ye are not your own? For ye are bought with a price: therefore glorify God in your body, and in your spirit, which are God's.

My Petition

Lord, my petition I make known,
Just like You said to do.
I boldly come before the throne
Having audience with You.

By invitation to receive
Your mercy and Your grace.
Finding everything I need,
Here in the secret place.

Under Your shadow, Lord Almighty;
Where I dwell and abide;
Above all principalities;
The refuge where I hide.

I ask for Your anointing,
Lord, let Your fire fall;
An oracle as You appoint me,
Set apart for Your call.

My honor and great privilege
To speak forth and decree,
Salvation, the gospel message
Unto all who will believe.

Scriptural Inspiration

1 John 5:14-15 And this is the confidence that we have in him, that, if we ask any thing according to his will, he heareth us: And if we know that he hear us, whatsoever we ask, we know that we have the petitions that we desired of him.

Hebrews 4:16 Let us therefore come boldly unto the throne of grace, that we may obtain mercy, and find grace to help in time of need.

Psalm 91:1-2 He that dwelleth in the secret place of the most High shall abide under the shadow of the Almighty. will say of the LORD, He is my refuge and my fortress: my God; in him will I trust.

Luke 3:16 John answered, saying unto them all, I indeed baptize you with water; but one mightier than I cometh, the latchet of whose shoes I am not worthy to unloose: he shall baptize you with the Holy Ghost and with fire:

1 Peter 4:11 If any man speak, let him speak as the oracles of God; if any man minister, let him do it as of the ability which God giveth: that God in all things may be glorified through Jesus Christ, to whom be praise and dominion for ever and ever. Amen.

2 Timothy 2:21 If a man therefore purge himself from these, he shall be a vessel unto honour, sanctified, and meet for the master's use, and prepared unto every good work.

Romans 1:16 For I am not ashamed of the gospel of Christ: for it is the power of God unto salvation to every one that believeth; to the Jew first, and also to the Greek.

My Portion

I bring into this present tense,
Provisions that you've made.
Confess Your Word with confidence,
Trusting in Your grace.

This shield of faith my great defence
And armor that You gave.
Your Word the sword of my offence,
The enemy to slay.

Your joy will always be my strength.
Perfect love makes my way;
Above all I could ask or think,
My portion for each day.

Lord, You supply all that we need,
Through life from faith to faith.
Your Word fulfilled as we receive,
Your provisions and Your grace.

Scriptural Inspiration

Romans 4:17 (As it is written, I have made thee a father of many nations,) before him whom he believed, even God, who quickeneth the dead, and calleth those things which be not as though they were.

Ephesians 5:1 Be ye therefore followers of God, as dear children;

Ephesians 6:13-17 Wherefore take unto you the whole armour of God, that ye may be able to withstand in the evil day, and having done all, to stand. Stand therefore, having your loins girt about with truth, and having on the breastplate of righteousness; And your feet shod with the preparation of the gospel of peace; Above all, taking the shield of faith, wherewith ye shall be able to quench all the fiery darts of the wicked. And take the helmet of salvation, and the sword of the Spirit, which is the word of God:

Nehemiah 8:10 Then he said unto them, Go your way, eat the fat, and drink the sweet, and send portions unto them for whom nothing is prepared: for this day is holy unto our Lord: neither be ye sorry; for the joy of the LORD is your strength.

Ephesians 3:20 Now unto him that is able to do exceeding abundantly above all that we ask or think, according to the power that worketh in us,

Philippians 4:19 But my God shall supply all your need according to his riches in glory by Christ Jesus.

Romans 1:17 For therein is the righteousness of God revealed from faith to faith: as it is written, The just shall live by faith.

Never Thirst Again

From the wells of your salvation,
Whoso will may quench their thirst.
Lord, by Your standing invitation,
Not by merit or by works.

By Your precious perfect love we live
Forever free from bonds of sin.
For by the water that You give,
We'll never thirst again.

Lord, You are worthy of all praise,
Our lives an offering to You.
Made righteous by Your love and grace,
Have Your way in all we do.

Inhabiting Your people's praise,
Your Glory in our midst.
We bow our hearts with our hands raised,
And receive Your precious gift.

Scriptural Inspiration

Isaiah 12:3 Therefore with joy shall ye draw water out of the wells of salvation.

Isaiah 55:1-3 Ho, every one that thirsteth, come ye to the waters, and he that hath no money; come ye, buy, and eat; yea, come, buy wine and milk without money and without price. Wherefore do ye spend money for that which is not bread? and your labour for that which satisfieth not? hearken diligently unto me, and eat ye that which is good, and let your soul delight itself in fatness. Incline your ear, and come unto me: hear, and your soul shall live; and I will make an everlasting covenant with you, even the sure mercies of David.

Galatians 2:16 Knowing that a man is not justified by the works of the law, but by the faith of Jesus Christ, even we have believed in Jesus Christ, that we might be justified by the faith of Christ, and not by the works of the law: for by the works of the law shall no flesh be justified.

John 4:14 But whosoever drinketh of the water that I shall give him shall never thirst; but the water that I shall give him shall be in him a well of water springing up into everlasting life.

2 Corinthians 5:21 For he hath made him to be sin for us, who knew no sin; that we might be made the righteousness of God in him.

Psalm 22:3 But thou art holy, O thou that inhabitest the praises of Israel.

Also see: **Romans 6:23** and **Ephesians Chpt 1**

Omniscient

Some challenges we must endure,
It's just a fact of life.
They build character that's for sure,
If we don't fall into strife.

Just count it all a joy, you know
When your faith is tried;
The value is much more than gold,
Though it be tried with fire.

The Lord knows what you're going through.
He's mindful of your needs.
He cares for each and every sparrow;
And for you much more than these!

Your very hairs are all numbered.
God is omniscient.
So walk by faith and stay under
His grace and covenant.

Scriptural Inspiration

Romans 5:3 And not only so, but we glory in tribulations also: knowing that tribulation worketh patience;

James 1:2-3 My brethren, count it all joy when ye fall into divers temptations; Knowing this, that the trying of your faith worketh patience.

1 Peter 1:7 That the trial of your faith, being much more precious than of gold that perisheth, though it be tried with fire, might be found unto praise and honour and glory at the appearing of Jesus Christ:

Matthew 6:8 Be not ye therefore like unto them: for your Father knoweth what things ye have need of, before ye ask him.

Matthew 10:29-30 Are not two sparrows sold for a farthing? and one of them shall not fall on the ground without your Father. But the very hairs of your head are all numbered.

Luke 12:7 But even the very hairs of your head are all numbered. Fear not therefore: ye are of more value than many sparrows.

1 John 3:20 For if our heart condemn us, God is greater than our heart, and knoweth all things.

Luke 12:30 For all these things do the nations of the world seek after: and your Father knoweth that ye have need of these things.

2 Corinthians 12:9 And he said unto me, My grace is sufficient for thee: for my strength is made perfect in weakness. Most gladly therefore will I rather glory in my infirmities, that the power of Christ may rest upon me.

Opinions

Some people claim that God says no!
In answer to their prayer;
The question looms if this is so,
Why do they pray in err?

If prayer is in line with God's Word
He never contradicts;
His promises always assured,
Unless we ask amiss.

As principles of order reign,
Like two plus two is four.
Foundations that will never change;
God's Word forever more.

No need to reinvent the wheel,
Or wring your hands and moan.
Truth isn't based on how you feel !
Those opinions are your own.

Scriptural Inspiration

1 John 5:15 And if we know that he hear us, whatsoever we ask, we know that we have the petitions that we desired of him.

Hebrews 4:16 Let us therefore come boldly unto the throne of grace, that we may obtain mercy, and find grace to help in time of need.

John 15:4-7 Abide in me, and I in you. As the branch cannot bear fruit of itself, except it abide in the vine; no more can ye, except ye abide in me. I am the vine, ye are the branches: He that abideth in me, and I in him, the same bringeth forth much fruit: for without me ye can do nothing. If a man abide not in me, he is cast forth as a branch, and is withered; and men gather them, and cast them into the fire, and they are burned. If ye abide in me, and my words abide in you, ye shall ask what ye will, and it shall be done unto you.

Mark 11:24 Therefore I say unto you, What things soever ye desire, when ye pray, believe that ye receive them, and ye shall have them.

2 Corinthians 1:20 For all the promises of God in him are yea, and in him Amen, unto the glory of God by us.

James 4:3 Ye ask, and receive not, because ye ask amiss, that ye may consume it upon your lusts.

Psalm 89:34 My covenant will I not break, nor alter the thing that is gone out of my lips.

Psalm 119:89 For ever, O LORD, thy word is settled in heaven.

Isaiah 55:8-11 For my thoughts are not your thoughts, neither are your ways my ways, saith the LORD. For as the heavens are higher than the earth, so are my ways higher than your ways, and my thoughts than your thoughts. For as the rain cometh down, and the snow from heaven, and returneth not thither, but watereth the earth, and maketh it bring forth and bud, that it may give seed to the sower, and bread to the eater: So shall my word be that goeth forth out of my mouth: it shall not return unto me void, but it shall accomplish that which I please, and it shall prosper in the thing whereto I sent it.

Order

Protocol must be observed,
In everything we do.
Ignoring this would be absurd,
Counterproductive too.

Order presides in God's design
In intricate detail.
For all creation this applies,
Perfection without fail.

Truth never contradicts itself,
Laws of logic verify.
Basic tenets of the Bible held,
Are safeguards against lies.

False narratives quickly exposed
By simple facts of truth.
Misinformation is a ploy
Of pathetic desperate fools.

Guard your heart and be prepared,
To give account of truth.
With love and kindness learn to share,
God's Word that's absolute.

Scriptural Inspiration

Ecclesiastes 3:1 To every thing there is a season, and a time to every purpose under the heaven:

Genesis 1:1 In the beginning God created the heaven and the earth. **(See all of chpt. 1)**

1 Peter 1:23-25 Being born again, not of corruptible seed, but of incorruptible, by the word of God, which liveth and abideth for ever. For all flesh is as grass, and all the glory of man as the flower of grass. The grass withereth, and the flower thereof falleth away: But the word of the Lord endureth for ever. And this is the word which by the gospel is preached unto you.

Psalm 119:89 For ever, O LORD, thy word is settled in heaven.

Psalm 89:34 My covenant will I not break, nor alter the thing that is gone out of my lips.

Matthew 24:35 Heaven and earth shall pass away, but my words shall not pass away.

2 Timothy 3:16-17 All scripture is given by inspiration of God, and is profitable for doctrine, for reproof, for correction, for instruction in righteousness: That the man of God may be perfect, throughly furnished unto all good works.

Proverbs 4:23 Keep thy heart with all diligence; for out of it are the issues of life.

2 Timothy 4:2-5 Preach the word; be instant in season, out of season; reprove, rebuke, exhort with all longsuffering and doctrine. For the time will come when they will not endure sound doctrine; but after their own lusts shall they heap to themselves teachers, having itching ears; And they shall turn away their ears from the truth, and shall be turned unto fables. But watch thou in all things, endure afflictions, do the work of an evangelist, make full proof of thy ministry.

Our Sustenance

Your Word carries Your anointing,
It is Your bond and seal.
Forever settled and unchanging,
Not based on how we feel.

Lord, You never alter anything
Spoken from Your lips.
Your covenants are guarantees
Sworn by Your Holiness.

Like every law and principle
Govern all that does exist.
Your Word presides as protocol,
It is our sustenance.

Lord, thank You for the certainty,
Of Your unchanging Word.
By faith we purpose to receive,
Your perfect Will, unobscured.

Scriptural Inspiration

Hebrews 4:12 For the word of God is quick, and powerful, and sharper than any twoedged sword, piercing even to the dividing asunder of soul and spirit, and of the joints and marrow, and is a discerner of the thoughts and intents of the heart.

Psalm 119:89 For ever, O LORD, thy word is settled in heaven.

2 Corinthians 5:7 (For we walk by faith, not by sight:)

Psalm 89:34 My covenant will I not break, nor alter the thing that is gone out of my lips.

Psalm 105:8-10 He hath remembered his covenant for ever, the word which he commanded to a thousand generations. Which covenant he made with Abraham, and his oath unto Isaac; And confirmed the same unto Jacob for a law, and to Israel for an everlasting covenant:

Hebrews 6:13 For when God made promise to Abraham, because he could swear by no greater, he sware by himself,

Matthew 4:4 But he answered and said, It is written, Man shall not live by bread alone, but by every word that proceedeth out of the mouth of God.

Matthew 5:17-18 Think not that I am come to destroy the law, or the prophets: I am not come to destroy, but to fulfil. For verily I say unto you, Till heaven and earth pass, one jot or one tittle shall in no wise pass from the law, till all be fulfilled.

Matthew 6:11-15 Give us this day our daily bread. And forgive us our debts, as we forgive our debtors. And lead us not into temptation, but deliver us from evil: For thine is the kingdom, and the power, and the glory, for ever. Amen. For if ye forgive men their trespasses, your heavenly Father will also forgive you: But if ye forgive not men their trespasses, neither will your Father forgive your trespasses.

Section Five

P - S

Pentecost	86
Perspective	88
Power of the Tongue	90
Redeemed from the Curse	92
Spiritual Things	94
Standard Weights and Measurements	96
Stop Apostasy	98
Storms	100
Such a Time as This	102
Sufficient	104

Pentecost

On the day of Pentecost,
In the upper room;
Not a person there was lost,
Jesus they all knew.

They waited for the Holy Ghost
As Jesus told them to;
The fire fell on each of those
Who came to be endued.

Anointed to fulfill His plans,
Empowered and equipped;
The same way all believers can
Receive this precious gift!

Believers saved and sanctified
Be filled to overflow,
Ask Jesus now to be baptized
In the Holy Ghost.

Scriptural Inspiration

Acts 2:1 And when the day of Pentecost was fully come, they were all with one accord in one place.

Luke 24:49 And, behold, I send the promise of my Father upon you: but tarry ye in the city of Jerusalem, until ye be endued with power from on high.

Acts 2:3-4 And there appeared unto them cloven tongues like as of fire, and it sat upon each of them. And they were all filled with the Holy Ghost, and began to speak with other tongues, as the Spirit gave them utterance.

Acts 4:31 And when they had prayed, the place was shaken where they were assembled together; and they were all filled with the Holy Ghost, and they spake the word of God with boldness.

Acts 2:39 For the promise is unto you, and to your children, and to all that are afar off, even as many as the Lord our God shall call.

Luke 3:16 John answered, saying unto them all, I indeed baptize you with water; but one mightier than I cometh, the latchet of whose shoes I am not worthy to unloose: he shall baptize you with the Holy Ghost and with fire:

Perspective

When sails are full, catching the breeze
And water's smooth as glass.
Blue skies far as the eye can see
And storms have long since past.

What occupies the heart of man,
Not driven by distress;
No urgency to make a stand,
Or trust God for success.

When everything is going well,
Do we still seek the Lord?
Do we press in? Are we compelled
To know Him more and more?

He takes no pleasure in our pain;
It's simply not His will.
But through our trials we often gain
Perspective that fulfills.

We cannot live by bread alone,
But by His every word.
His perfect will for us made known,
His perfect love assured.

Jeremiah 17:9 The heart is deceitful above all things, and desperately wicked: who can know it?

Matthew 24:36, 42 But of that day and hour knoweth no man, no, not the angels of heaven, but my Father only. Watch therefore: for ye know not what hour your Lord doth come.

1 Thessalonians 5:1-6 But of the times and the seasons, brethren, ye have no need that I write unto you. For yourselves know perfectly that the day of the Lord so cometh as a thief in the night. For when they shall say, Peace and safety; then sudden destruction cometh upon them, as travail upon a woman with child; and they shall not escape. But ye, brethren, are not in darkness, that that day should overtake you as a thief. Ye are all the children of light, and the children of the day: we are not of the night, nor of darkness. Therefore let us not sleep, as do others; but let us watch and be sober.

Isaiah 55:6 Seek ye the LORD while he may be found, call ye upon him while he is near:

James 4:8 Draw nigh to God, and he will draw nigh to you. Cleanse your hands, ye sinners; and purify your hearts, ye double minded.

1 Peter 1:6-7 Wherein ye greatly rejoice, though now for a season, if need be, ye are in heaviness through manifold temptations: That the trial of your faith, being much more precious than of gold that perisheth, though it be tried with fire, might be found unto praise and honour and glory at the appearing of Jesus Christ:

1 Peter 4:12 Beloved, think it not strange concerning the fiery trial which is to try you, as though some strange thing happened unto you:

James 1:13 Let no man say when he is tempted, I am tempted of God: for God cannot be tempted with evil, neither tempteth he any man:

Matthew 4:4 But he answered and said, It is written, Man shall not live by bread alone, but by every word that proceedeth out of the mouth of God.

Power of the Tongue

Death and life are in the tongue,
Power in what we say.
Read Proverbs eighteen, twenty one.
God created us this way.

See Mark eleven, twenty three,
We'll have what we say.
It's important, what we believe,
For thus our words portray.

Search it out, see for yourself;
This is by God's design.
What we believe and confess
Is destiny defined.

Before you now is death or life;
The choice is yours to make.
Receive God's Word and testify,
Your destiny awaits.

"We use words to express what we believe…
We set the course of our destiny by the words we speak." –mg

Proverbs 18:21 Death and life are in the power of the tongue: and they that love it shall eat the fruit thereof.

Romans 10:9 That if thou shalt confess with thy mouth the Lord Jesus, and shalt believe in thine heart that God hath raised him from the dead, thou shalt be saved.

Mark 11:23 For verily I say unto you, That whosoever shall say unto this mountain, Be thou removed, and be thou cast into the sea; and shall not doubt in his heart, but shall believe that those things which he saith shall come to pass, he shall have whatsoever he saith.

Mark 11:23 (NKJV) For assuredly, I say to you, whoever says to this mountain, 'Be removed and cast into the sea,' and does not doubt in his heart, but believes that those things he says will be done, he will have whatever he says.

Matthew 12:37 For by thy words thou shall be justified, and by thy words thou shalt be condemned.

Redeemed from the Curse

Missing the mark is sin defined,
Like arrows fly astray;
So it is with all mankind,
God's mark is unattained.

There is a curse by sin consigned,
Deuteronomy 28.
So Jesus came to justify
And save us by His grace.

All redeemed who belong to Christ
The curse is not our fate;
Galatians three verse 29
Perfect love took our place.

Read through Galatians 3 and find
Your inheritance today.
Be transformed, renew your mind,
To what God has to say!

"That you may prove what is that good and acceptable and perfect will of God." *Romans 12:1,2*

Romans 3:23 For all have sinned, and come short of the glory of God;

Deuteronomy 28:1-2, 15 And it shall come to pass, if thou shalt hearken diligently unto the voice of the LORD thy God, to observe and to do all his commandments which I command thee this day, that the LORD thy God will set thee on high above all nations of the earth: And all these blessings shall come on thee, and overtake thee, if thou shalt hearken unto the voice of the LORD thy God. ... But it shall come to pass, if thou wilt not hearken unto the voice of the LORD thy God, to observe to do all his commandments and his statutes which I command thee this day; that all these curses shall come upon thee, and overtake thee:

Galatians 3:13-14, 29 Christ hath redeemed us from the curse of the law, being made a curse for us: for it is written, Cursed is every one that hangeth on a tree: That the blessing of Abraham might come on the Gentiles through Jesus Christ; that we might receive the promise of the Spirit through faith. ... And if ye be Christ's, then are ye Abraham's seed, and heirs according to the promise.

Spiritual Things

All things are working for my good,
No matter how it seems.
God said to trust Him and He would
Fulfill His word in me.

Spiritual things can't be discerned
With the natural mind;
But He reveals what can't be learned,
In seeking Him we find.

If we knock the door will open;
Ask and you shall receive.
As we simply place our hope in
What God said, and believe.

With His word, which is anointed,
Mountains move and giants fall;
For in Christ we are appointed
More than conquerors in all.

Scriptural Inspiration

Romans 8:28 And we know that all things work together for good to them that love God, to them who are the called according to his purpose.

1 Corinthians 2:14 But the natural man receiveth not the things of the Spirit of God: for they are foolishness unto him: neither can he know them, because they are spiritually discerned.

Matthew 7:7 Ask, and it shall be given you; seek, and ye shall find; knock, and it shall be opened unto you:

Romans 8:37 Nay, in all these things we are more than conquerors through him that loved us.

Standard Weights and Measurements

Consider weights and measurements,
Like shekels long ago;
A standard weight that represents
Fair trade for all to know.

These weights must always be the same,
Impartial for the scale.
This set amount a shekel weighs
Measures the price of sale.

The Hebrew word for *righteousness*
Is pronounced Sid-Ah-Ka;
"According to standard" is the gist of this,
As in Genesis 15:6 (selah).

God's standard for righteousness
Absolute and precise;
For sin there's zero tolerance,
On scales that cannot lie.

The standard so impossible
For mankind to attain;
Perfect love so inexhaustible
Through Jesus made a way.

Scriptural Inspiration

Genesis 23:16 And Abraham hearkened unto Ephron; and Abraham weighed to Ephron the silver, which he had named in the audience of the sons of Heth, four hundred shekels of silver, current money with the merchant.

Leviticus 19:36 Just balances, just weights, a just ephah, and a just hin, shall ye have: I am the LORD your God, which brought you out of the land of Egypt.

Deuteronomy 25:15-16 But thou shalt have a perfect and just weight, a perfect and just measure shalt thou have: that thy days may be lengthened in the land which the LORD thy God giveth thee. For all that do such things, and all that do unrighteously, are an abomination unto the LORD thy God.

Micah 6:11 Shall I count them pure with the wicked balances, and with the bag of deceitful weights?

Proverbs 20:10 Divers weights, and divers measures, both of them are alike abomination to the LORD.

Genesis 15:6 And he believed in the LORD; and he counted it to him for righteousness.

Romans 3:20 Therefore by the deeds of the law there shall no flesh be justified in his sight: for by the law is the knowledge of sin.

Psalm 24:3-4 Who shall ascend into the hill of the LORD? or who shall stand in his holy place? He that hath clean hands, and a pure heart; who hath not lifted up his soul unto vanity, nor sworn deceitfully.

Galatians 2:16 Knowing that a man is not justified by the works of the law, but by the faith of Jesus Christ, even we have believed in Jesus Christ, that we might be justified by the faith of Christ, and not by the works of the law: for by the works of the law shall no flesh be justified.

Stop Apostasy

If you're ashamed of what God said
And compromise His Word,
Preaching what you think instead,
From opinions so absurd;

The day will come, a price to pay
For what you've said and done;
For every soul you've led astray,
You'll answer for each one!

The message of the Gospel is
The truth that sets them free.
The power of God by which we live
To all who will believe.

All other ground is sinking sand,
Lies sent to destroy!
Keep people from the promised land
And steal their peace and joy.

An evil heart of unbelief,
Stop talking like the world;
God's Word is what you're called to preach!
Consider yourself warned!

Scriptural Inspiration

Galatians 1:7-12 Which is not another; but there be some that trouble you, and would pervert the gospel of Christ. But though we, or an angel from heaven, preach any other gospel unto you than that which we have preached unto you, let him be accursed. As we said before, so say I now again, If any man preach any other gospel unto you than that ye have received, let him be accursed. For do I now persuade men, or God? or do I seek to please men? for if I yet pleased men, I should not be the servant of Christ. But I certify you, brethren, that the gospel which was preached of me is not after man. For I neither received it of man, neither was I taught it, but by the revelation of Jesus Christ.

2 Timothy 3:5 Having a form of godliness, but denying the power thereof: from such turn away.

Revelation 22:18 For I testify unto every man that heareth the words of the prophecy of this book, If any man shall add unto these things, God shall add unto him the plagues that are written in this book:

Romans 1:16 For I am not ashamed of the gospel of Christ: for it is the power of God unto salvation to every one that believeth; to the Jew first, and also to the Greek.

Hebrews 3:12 Take heed, brethren, lest there be in any of you an evil heart of unbelief, in departing from the living God.

2 Peter 1:16-21 For we have not followed cunningly devised fables, when we made known unto you the power and coming of our Lord Jesus Christ, but were eyewitnesses of his majesty. For he received from God the Father honour and glory, when there came such a voice to him from the excellent glory, This is my beloved Son, in whom I am well pleased. And this voice which came from heaven we heard, when we were with him in the holy mount. We have also a more sure word of prophecy; whereunto ye do well that ye take heed, as unto a light that shineth in a dark place, until the day dawn, and the day star arise in your hearts: Knowing this first, that no prophecy of the scripture is of any private interpretation. For the prophecy came not in old time by the will of man: but holy men of God spake as they were moved by the Holy Ghost.

Storms

In this world there will be storms,
But God is not to blame.
Renew your mind, be not conformed
To this world's thoughts and ways.

Trust the Lord before the storm,
His Word will build your faith.
Renew your mind and be transformed,
To prove God's will today.

The Word of God will calm the storm
Or take you through unscathed;
But only if you trust the Lord,
His Word, His Truth, His Grace.

So if you're ever in a storm
Don't believe the lies that say,
It must be God that caused the storm...
For yourself investigate!

Read Deuteronomy chpt 28, then Galatians chpt 3
(Gal. 3:13, 14, 29 are referring to Deut 28)
Next read Psalms 89:34; Hebrews 6:12-18; 1 John 5:4; James chpt 1; Numbers 23:19.
Actually, the entire Word of God reveals His heart for you. Perfect love is the deliverer; Not the source of the storm.

John 16:33 These things I have spoken unto you, that in me ye might have peace. In the world ye shall have tribulation: but be of good cheer; I have overcome the world.

Romans 12:2 And be not conformed to this world: but be ye transformed by the renewing of your mind, that ye may prove what is that good, and acceptable, and perfect, will of God.

Romans 10:17 So then faith cometh by hearing, and hearing by the word of God.

James 1:13 Let no man say when he is tempted, I am tempted of God: for God cannot be tempted with evil, neither tempteth he any man:

Such a Time as This

You must focus your attention
On things I've planned for you;
Time is short, and there are some
Important things to do.

Your abilities will come short,
My strength will see you through.
Hear my voice, trust my report
In all I'll have you do.

Don't be concerned with how it seems,
Let me be in control.
My will be done as you decree,
Where I send you must go.

With healing and deliverance,
My power to display;
Prepared for such a time as this,
I called you for this day.

(See Romans chpt 8)

Proverbs 3:5-6 Trust in the LORD with all thine heart; and lean not unto thine own understanding. In all thy ways acknowledge him, and he shall direct thy paths.

(See Hebrews chpt 3 & 4)

Mark 16:17-18 And these signs shall follow them that believe; In my name shall they cast out devils; they shall speak with new tongues; They shall take up serpents; and if they drink any deadly thing, it shall not hurt them; they shall lay hands on the sick, and they shall recover.

Sufficient

Sufficient is Your grace for me
Through challenges I face.
You're mindful of my every need
And every step I take.

So I resist anxieties
For this is Your command.
Because You said You'll care for me,
I leave them in Your hands.

You're not a man that You can lie,
Your Word is absolute.
I walk by faith and not by sight
By simply trusting you.

Through the dark and stormy night,
With devastation near.
Lord, by Your grace we'll be all right.
In you, I have no fear.

Scriptural Inspiration

2 Corinthians 12:9 And he said unto me, My grace is sufficient for thee: for my strength is made perfect in weakness. Most gladly therefore will I rather glory in my infirmities, that the power of Christ may rest upon me.

Matthew 6:8 Be not ye therefore like unto them: for your Father knoweth what things ye have need of, before ye ask him.

Philippians 4:6 Be careful for nothing; but in every thing by prayer and supplication with thanksgiving let your requests be made known unto God.

Matthew 11:28-30 Come unto me, all ye that labour and are heavy laden, and I will give you rest. Take my yoke upon you, and learn of me; for I am meek and lowly in heart: and ye shall find rest unto your souls. For my yoke is easy, and my burden is light.

1 Peter 5:7 Casting all your care upon him; for he careth for you.

Numbers 23:19 God is not a man, that he should lie; neither the son of man, that he should repent: hath he said, and shall he not do it? or hath he spoken, and shall he not make it good?

Psalm 89:34 My covenant will I not break, nor alter the thing that is gone out of my lips.

Hebrews 13:8 Jesus Christ the same yesterday, and to day, and for ever.

James 1:17 Every good gift and every perfect gift is from above, and cometh down from the Father of lights, with whom is no variableness, neither shadow of turning.

2 Corinthians 5:7 (For we walk by faith, not by sight:)

2 Timothy 1:7 For God hath not given us the spirit of fear; but of power, and of love, and of a sound mind.

Section Six

T - Z

The Broadcast	108
The Gift	110
The Gospel	112
The Hoax	114
The Premise	116
The Prize	118
The Snake Line	120
Together Once Again	122
Training Wheels	124
Trust the Lord	126
Truth	128
Victory or Defeat	130
What Can't Be Done	132
Your Word	134

The Broadcast

It resonates within my heart,
Sustains me day by day.
The counsel Perfect Love imparts,
That guides and makes my way.

Broadcast throughout eternity,
The signal strong and clear;
God sent His Word to set you free,
Have you tuned in to hear?

Like dialing in a radio
To find the frequency.
You must choose, you're in control,
Turn the dial 'til you receive!

The Word of God, the Bread of Life,
A Lamp unto our feet.
Expressly given and inspired
By God to you and me.

Scriptural Inspiration

Proverbs 3:5-6 Trust in the LORD with all thine heart; and lean not unto thine own understanding. In all thy ways acknowledge him, and he shall direct thy paths.

John 8:36 If the Son therefore shall make you free, ye shall be free indeed.

John 6:35 And Jesus said unto them, I am the bread of life: he that cometh to me shall never hunger; and he that believeth on me shall never thirst.

John 6:48 I am that bread of life.

Psalm 119:105 Thy word is a lamp unto my feet, and a light unto my path.

2 Timothy 3:16 All scripture is given by inspiration of God, and is profitable for doctrine, for reproof, for correction, for instruction in righteousness:

The Gift

Thank You, Lord, my name is written,
In the Lamb's Book of Life.
This greatest gift ever given,
Salvation makes us right.

Redeemed from the sin condition
By Jesus our dear Savior.
Thank You, Lord, for Your provision
Of unmerited favor.

As we believe You with our heart,
By mouth confession made...
Receive the gift that You impart
And enter in Your grace.

You are my Lord, preeminent.
And I am not my own.
Forever Yours by covenant
That perfect love atoned.

Scriptural Inspiration

Revelation 21:27 And there shall in no wise enter into it any thing that defileth, neither whatsoever worketh abomination, or maketh a lie: but they which are written in the Lamb's book of life.

Romans 1:16 For I am not ashamed of the gospel of Christ: for it is the power of God unto salvation to every one that believeth; to the Jew first, and also to the Greek.

Galatians 3:13-14 Christ hath redeemed us from the curse of the law, being made a curse for us: for it is written, Cursed is every one that hangeth on a tree: That the blessing of Abraham might come on the Gentiles through Jesus Christ; that we might receive the promise of the Spirit through faith.

John 3:15-19 That whosoever believeth in him should not perish, but have eternal life. For God so loved the world, that he gave his only begotten Son, that whosoever believeth in him should not perish, but have everlasting life. For God sent not his Son into the world to condemn the world; but that the world through him might be saved. He that believeth on him is not condemned: but he that believeth not is condemned already, because he hath not believed in the name of the only begotten Son of God. And this is the condemnation, that light is come into the world, and men loved darkness rather than light, because their deeds were evil.

Romans 10:9 That if thou shalt confess with thy mouth the Lord Jesus, and shalt believe in thine heart that God hath raised him from the dead, thou shalt be saved.

1 Corinthians 6:19-20 What? know ye not that your body is the temple of the Holy Ghost which is in you, which ye have of God, and ye are not your own? For ye are bought with a price: therefore glorify God in your body, and in your spirit, which are God's.

The Gospel

Unchanging everlasting truth,
The gospel is good news.
Immutable and absolute,
Perfect Love's desire for you.

His plans beyond all you could dream
Are yours if you'll receive,
The gift of life eternally,
If only you believe.

The gospel message of salvation,
The power of God to save;
Since before the world's foundation,
The plan that Jesus made.

His finished work at Calvary
Fulfilled redemption plan.
Exonerates and makes us clean
As only Jesus can.

Romans 1:16 For I am not ashamed of the gospel of Christ: for it is the power of God unto salvation to every one that believeth; to the Jew first, and also to the Greek.

Luke 4:18 The Spirit of the Lord is upon me, because he hath anointed me to preach the gospel to the poor; he hath sent me to heal the brokenhearted, to preach deliverance to the captives, and recovering of sight to the blind, to set at liberty them that are bruised,

Ephesians 3:20 Now unto him that is able to do exceeding abundantly above all that we ask or think, according to the power that worketh in us,

Ephesians 1:4 According as he hath chosen us in him before the foundation of the world, that we should be holy and without blame before him in love:

1 Peter 1:20 Who verily was foreordained before the foundation of the world, but was manifest in these last times for you,

Revelation 13:8 And all that dwell upon the earth shall worship him, whose names are not written in the book of life of the Lamb slain from the foundation of the world.

Hebrews 4:3 For we which have believed do enter into rest, as he said, As I have sworn in my wrath, if they shall enter into my rest: although the works were finished from the foundation of the world.

1 Timothy 2:5 For there is one God, and one mediator between God and men, the man Christ Jesus;

The Hoax

We observe in every realm
How order does preside.
Principles that govern well,
All by God's design.

Creation is so intricate,
Inexhaustible detail
Man hasn't scratched the surface yet
Of fulcrums that prevail.

The big bang is ridiculous!
A theory that's absurd.
Fools perpetrate such lies on us,
As if by science learned.

Like evolution, the big hoax,
Made up in spite of facts;
Misinformation's not a joke,
It's an outright attack!

They tell our children there's no God
And truth's not absolute.
But the evil that's behind this plot
Will ultimately lose!

Scriptural Inspiration

Romans 1:16 For I am not ashamed of the gospel of Christ: for it is the power of God unto salvation to every one that believeth; to the Jew first, and also to the Greek.

Luke 4:18 The Spirit of the Lord is upon me, because he hath anointed me to preach the gospel to the poor; he hath sent me to heal the brokenhearted, to preach deliverance to the captives, and recovering of sight to the blind, to set at liberty them that are bruised,

Ephesians 3:20 Now unto him that is able to do exceeding abundantly above all that we ask or think, according to the power that worketh in us,

Ephesians 1:4 According as he hath chosen us in him before the foundation of the world, that we should be holy and without blame before him in love:

1 Peter 1:20 Who verily was foreordained before the foundation of the world, but was manifest in these last times for you,

Revelation 13:8 And all that dwell upon the earth shall worship him, whose names are not written in the book of life of the Lamb slain from the foundation of the world.

Hebrews 4:3 For we which have believed do enter into rest, as he said, As I have sworn in my wrath, if they shall enter into my rest: although the works were finished from the foundation of the world.

1 Timothy 2:5 For there is one God, and one mediator between God and men, the man Christ Jesus;

Revelation 20:3 And cast him into the bottomless pit, and shut him up, and set a seal upon him, that he should deceive the nations no more, till the thousand years should be fulfilled: and after that he must be loosed a little season.

The Premise

Success is not by accident
But principles applied.
Develop skills by hours spent
And willingness to try.

Not random but deliberate
With effort that's intense.
What you put in is what you get,
It only makes good sense.

This order that we recognize
And all through life we see,
Success is rarely a surprise,
What we sow we reap.

So, considering this premise
To desired results attained;
Don't come short of God's promises,
Spiritual principles work the same!

2 Corinthians 9:6 But this I say, He which soweth sparingly shall reap also sparingly; and he which soweth bountifully shall reap also bountifully.

Galatians 6:7 Be not deceived; God is not mocked: for whatsoever a man soweth, that shall he also reap.

Hebrews 3:10-12, 19 Wherefore I was grieved with that generation, and said, They do alway err in their heart; and they have not known my ways. So I sware in my wrath, They shall not enter into my rest.) Take heed, brethren, lest there be in any of you an evil heart of unbelief, in departing from the living God. ... So we see that they could not enter in because of unbelief.

Hebrews 4:1-2 Let us therefore fear, lest, a promise being left us of entering into his rest, any of you should seem to come short of it. For unto us was the gospel preached, as well as unto them: but the word preached did not profit them, not being mixed with faith in them that heard it.

The Prize

Keep pressing on toward the prize,
The highest call in life.
To preach The Word uncompromised
And do all things through Christ.

This treasure is to be baptized,
With the Holy Ghost and Fire.
Set apart and sanctified,
To have the mind of Christ.

Our Comforter and Paraclete
Enables and equips.
By His anointing we can see
The working of His gifts.

The branch itself cannot bear fruit,
For life comes through the vine;
And so for us the same is true,
In Christ we must abide.

Scriptural Inspiration

Philippians 3:14 I press toward the mark for the prize of the high calling of God in Christ Jesus.

Philippians 4:11 Not that I speak in respect of want: for I have learned, in whatsoever state I am, therewith to be content.

2 Corinthians 4:7 But we have this treasure in earthen vessels, that the excellency of the power may be of God, and not of us.

Matthew 3:11 I indeed baptize you with water unto repentance: but he that cometh after me is mightier than I, whose shoes I am not worthy to bear: he shall baptize you with the Holy Ghost and with fire:

1 Corinthians 2:16 For who hath known the mind of the Lord, that he may instruct him? But we have the mind of Christ.

John 14:16, 26 And I will pray the Father, and he shall give you another Comforter, that he may abide with you for ever; ... But the Comforter, which is the Holy Ghost, whom the Father will send in my name, he shall teach you all things, and bring all things to your remembrance, whatsoever I have said unto you.

John 15:26 But when the Comforter is come, whom I will send unto you from the Father, even the Spirit of truth, which proceedeth from the Father, he shall testify of me:

1 Corinthians 12:11 But all these worketh that one and the selfsame Spirit, dividing to every man severally as he will.

John 15:4-7 Abide in me, and I in you. As the branch cannot bear fruit of itself, except it abide in the vine; no more can ye, except ye abide in me.   I am the vine, ye are the branches: He that abideth in me, and I in him, the same bringeth forth much fruit: for without me ye can do nothing. If a man abide not in me, he is cast forth as a branch, and is withered; and men gather them, and cast them into the fire, and they are burned. If ye abide in me, and my words abide in you, ye shall ask what ye will, and it shall be done unto you.

The Snake Line

A certain place called the snake line,
Beyond which snakes don't go;
In elevations that are high.
An interesting fact to know.

If anyone by chance should climb
Above this line it's shown,
Venomous snakes they will not find,
For serpents stay below.

One place a similar truth applies,
That we should also know...
The presence of the Lord provides
Sanctuary from all foes.

Press in to Christ, in Him abide;
Where evil cannot go.
Rise high and become energized,
To run this race below.

Psalm 18:2 The LORD is my rock, and my fortress, and my deliverer; my God, my strength, in whom I will trust; my buckler, and the horn of my salvation, and my high tower.

Psalm 16:11 Thou wilt shew me the path of life: in thy presence is fulness of joy; at thy right hand there are pleasures for evermore.

Hebrews 12:1 Wherefore seeing we also are compassed about with so great a cloud of witnesses, let us lay aside every weight, and the sin which doth so easily beset us, and let us run with patience the race that is set before us,

Together Once Again

Of all the things that we hold dear
The things we cherish most,
The list gets smaller year by year,
By perspective, I suppose.

This temporal realm is quickly gone
And so we recognize
Our time spent here is not too long,
Then comes the greatest prize.

Eternal life by God's design,
Through Jesus Christ our Lord.
A destiny beyond all time,
Imagine what's in store…

When we get to the promised land,
Where joy shall never end.
I'll look for you, to hold your hand,
Together once again.

2 Corinthians 4:18   While we look not at the things which are seen, but at the things which are not seen: for the things which are seen are temporal; but the things which are not seen are eternal.

James 4:14   Whereas ye know not what shall be on the morrow. For what is your life? It is even a vapour, that appeareth for a little time, and then vanisheth away.

1 Corinthians 2:9   But as it is written, Eye hath not seen, nor ear heard, neither have entered into the heart of man, the things which God hath prepared for them that love him.

John 3:16   For God so loved the world, that he gave his only begotten Son, that whosoever believeth in him should not perish, but have everlasting life.

Psalm 16:11   Thou wilt shew me the path of life: in thy presence is fulness of joy; at thy right hand there are pleasures for evermore.

1 Thessalonians 4:13-18   But I would not have you to be ignorant, brethren, concerning them which are asleep, that ye sorrow not, even as others which have no hope. For if we believe that Jesus died and rose again, even so them also which sleep in Jesus will God bring with him. For this we say unto you by the word of the Lord, that we which are alive and remain unto the coming of the Lord shall not prevent them which are asleep. For the Lord himself shall descend from heaven with a shout, with the voice of the archangel, and with the trump of God: and the dead in Christ shall rise first: Then we which are alive and remain shall be caught up together with them in the clouds, to meet the Lord in the air: and so shall we ever be with the Lord. Wherefore comfort one another with these words.

Training Wheels

The training wheels that helped us learn
Came off after a while;
With practice we became experts,
Developed skills by trial.

But how funny it would be to see
Grown-ups with trainers on;
Yet many Christians still have need
They've never moved beyond.

Training wheels and safety nets,
With no desire to grow.
Foundations laid have no effect,
Still on the milk alone.

Our mandate is to walk by faith,
Trust God with all our heart;
Lest we come short, a promise made,
His rest would be our part.

1 Corinthians 13:11 When I was a child, I spake as a child, I understood as a child, I thought as a child: but when I became a man, I put away childish things.

Hebrews 6:1 Therefore leaving the principles of the doctrine of Christ, let us go on unto perfection; not laying again the foundation of repentance from dead works, and of faith toward God,

Hebrews 5:11-14 Of whom we have many things to say, and hard to be uttered, seeing ye are dull of hearing. For when for the time ye ought to be teachers, ye have need that one teach you again which be the first principles of the oracles of God; and are become such as have need of milk, and not of strong meat. For every one that useth milk is unskilful in the word of righteousness: for he is a babe. But strong meat belongeth to them that are of full age, even those who by reason of use have their senses exercised to discern both good and evil.

Romans 1:17 For therein is the righteousness of God revealed from faith to faith: as it is written, The just shall live by faith.

Hebrews 10:38 Now the just shall live by faith: but if any man draw back, my soul shall have no pleasure in him.

Hebrews 4:1 Let us therefore fear, lest, a promise being left us of entering into his rest, any of you should seem to come short of it.

Trust the Lord

When skies are dark and threatening,
You don't know what to do;
So ominous you dread the thing,
That's closing in on you.

And if there seems to be no way,
How will you make it through?
This is the time when you must say,
Lord, I place my trust in You.

Believe the Word that's absolute,
Given to us by the Lord.
Declare His covenant made for you,
It will not come back void.

The Name that is above all names,
Jesus gave us to use,
To speak forth His Word and proclaim,
His plans fulfilled in you.

2 Timothy 1:7 For God hath not given us the spirit of fear; but of power, and of love, and of a sound mind.

Philippians 4:8 Finally, brethren, whatsoever things are true, whatsoever things are honest, whatsoever things are just, whatsoever things are pure, whatsoever things are lovely, whatsoever things are of good report; if there be any virtue, and if there be any praise, think on these things.

Isaiah 55:11 So shall my word be that goeth forth out of my mouth: it shall not return unto me void, but it shall accomplish that which I please, and it shall prosper in the thing whereto I sent it.

Ephesians 1:19-21 And what is the exceeding greatness of his power to us-ward who believe, according to the working of his mighty power, Which he wrought in Christ, when he raised him from the dead, and set him at his own right hand in the heavenly places, Far above all principality, and power, and might, and dominion, and every name that is named, not only in this world, but also in that which is to come:

Philippians 2:9 Wherefore God also hath highly exalted him, and given him a name which is above every name:

Psalm 138:2 I will worship toward thy holy temple, and praise thy name for thy lovingkindness and for thy truth: for thou hast magnified thy word above all thy name.

Truth

Information shapes each worldview
How we perceive this life.
What we think and choose to do,
Even impacts our sight.

Yes, our worldviews important things,
Yet *all* not based on truth!
The information source can bring
Perception that's askew.

Absolute truth is *not* subjective,
Opinions come and go.
Truth is exclusive and objective,
For all who seek to know.

Use caution, always verify
The information source.
Resist, reject the very lies
Intended to destroy.

Your perception is reality
That you operate within;
Be sure by truth it came to be,
Your destiny depends.

Scriptural Inspiration

Romans 10:14 How then shall they call on him in whom they have not believed? and how shall they believe in him of whom they have not heard? and how shall they hear without a preacher?

Matthew 13:15 For this people's heart is waxed gross, and their ears are dull of hearing, and their eyes they have closed; lest at any time they should see with their eyes, and hear with their ears, and should understand with their heart, and should be converted, and I should heal them.

John 14:6 Jesus saith unto him, I am the way, the truth, and the life: no man cometh unto the Father, but by me.

Matthew 7:7 Ask, and it shall be given you; seek, and ye shall find; knock, and it shall be opened unto you:

Deuteronomy 11:16 Take heed to yourselves, that your heart be not deceived, and ye turn aside, and serve other gods, and worship them;

John 8:32 And ye shall know the truth, and the truth shall make you free.

Victory or Defeat

When you're facing trials and troubles
And you see no way out,
Don't allow your faith to crumble;
That's what this is about!

Every test will make you stronger,
Press on and you will grow.
Stay in the Word a little longer,
Faith comes by what you know.

What's in your heart is what you'll speak,
It reflects what you believe.
Therein is victory or defeat,
For it affects what you receive.

Aline yourself with what God says,
Agree with Him alone.
For you will have what you confess;
His plans, or your own.

John 16:33 These things I have spoken unto you, that in me ye might have peace. In the world ye shall have tribulation: but be of good cheer; I have overcome the world.

Romans 10:17 So then faith cometh by hearing, and hearing by the word of God.

Luke 6:45 A good man out of the good treasure of his heart bringeth forth that which is good; and an evil man out of the evil treasure of his heart bringeth forth that which is evil: for of the abundance of the heart his mouth speaketh.

Mark 11:23 For verily I say unto you, That whosoever shall say unto this mountain, Be thou removed, and be thou cast into the sea; and shall not doubt in his heart, but shall believe that those things which he saith shall come to pass; he shall have whatsoever he saith.

Matthew 12:37 For by thy words thou shalt be justified, and by thy words thou shalt be condemned.

What Can't Be Done

When Peter said, Lord, bid me come,
His eyes were on the Lord.
Then Peter did what can't be done,
When he climbed overboard.

Actually walked on water some,
Till his eyes got on the storm.
From having faith to having none,
He cried out, Save me, Lord!

Life's challenges are all the same,
Perception is the key;
God's word for you will never change,
It's yours if you believe.

Wherever Jesus bids you come,
Nevermind the storms;
Empowered to do what can't be done,
If your eyes stay on the Lord.

Scriptural Inspiration

Matthew 14:28-33 And Peter answered him and said, Lord, if it be thou, bid me come unto thee on the water. And he said, Come. And when Peter was come down out of the ship, he walked on the water, to go to Jesus. But when he saw the wind boisterous, he was afraid; and beginning to sink, he cried, saying, Lord, save me. And immediately Jesus stretched forth his hand, and caught him, and said unto him, O thou of little faith, wherefore didst thou doubt? And when they were come into the ship, the wind ceased. Then they that were in the ship came and worshipped him, saying, Of a truth thou art the Son of God.

Mark 9:23 Jesus said unto him, If thou canst believe, all things are possible to him that believeth.

Philippians 3:14 I press toward the mark for the prize of the high calling of God in Christ Jesus.

Your Word

Your Word reveals to us your heart,
The very source of life.
The essence, Lord, of who You are,
Perfect Love personified.

It's impossible to separate
Your Word from who You are,
The same sustains and did create
Galaxies beyond the stars.

By Your Word all things consist.
Our being is in You.
Unsearchable and limitless,
You preside, Lord, absolute.

Beyond description or compare,
More than we comprehend;
Father, Your perfect love and care
Is our portion without end.
  Hallelujah !

Scriptural Inspiration

John 1:1-4 In the beginning was the Word, and the Word was with God, and the Word was God. The same was in the beginning with God. All things were made by him; and without him was not any thing made that was made. In him was life; and the life was the light of men.

Colossians 1:17 And he is before all things, and by him all things consist.

Acts 17:28 For in him we live, and move, and have our being; as certain also of your own poets have said, For we are also his offspring.

Romans 11:33 O the depth of the riches both of the wisdom and knowledge of God! how unsearchable are his judgments, and his ways past finding out!

1 John 4:16 And we have known and believed the love that God hath to us. God is love; and he that dwelleth in love dwelleth in God, and God in him.

Critical Thinking

As a minister commissioned to bring you this message, the first thing I want you to know is "God is not mad at you." God is not looking for ways to punish you or set you up for something horrible to teach you a lesson!

In some religious circles, you may hear nonsense like that. But that's all it is—religious nonsense. If you would like to know how God really feels about you, read His love letter to you, the Bible. You will be thrilled to learn some very good news! That's what the Gospel is: "Good News."

In God's Word, He reveals His perfect love for you and His desire for you to be in a right relationship with Him. Just read **the 1st chapter of John** to see how He sent His Word to redeem humankind. Then open your Bible to **2 Corinthians 5:19,21** and find out what perfect Love did to reconcile a lost humanity. If you would like to see the "big picture" and come to a clear understanding of God's plans and provisions for you, read what The Holy Spirit inspired Paul to write to the church at Rome. (**The New Testament book of Romans**). Read it again and again if need be, until it settles into your heart just how much our Heavenly Father cares about you. This will forever change your perception, and position you to receive His perfect Love, His perfect plans, and His perfect provisions.

Before moving on with the exposition of "Understanding Life's Narrative," I would like to touch on two essential foundational points that will refute more nonsense and fallacies. These points are the very basis of everything else in this presentation, in this book, and, *actually in all pertaining to our destiny.* Everything squarely rests upon these absolute and profound truths:

1. <u>**God's plan of Salvation is exclusive.**</u>
   (All roads do NOT lead to eternal life).

   - **1 Timothy 2:5:** *For there is one God, and one mediator between God and men, the man Christ Jesus;*
   - **John 14:6**: *Jesus saith unto him, I am the way, the truth, and the life: no man cometh unto the Father, but by me.*

"Truth is narrow and exclusive by it's very definition. And those who proclaim truth may be accused of being narrowminded."

Nevertheless, by the discipline of Critical Thinking, there are Laws of Logic that simply make fallacies irrelevant, even absurd! Rational presuppositions are built upon logical absolutes. Without recognition of absolute truth, nonsense will be rampant.

Here are three fundamental Laws of Logic:

- <u>The Law of Identity</u>
  Something identified is what it is... not something else.
- <u>The Law of Non-Contradiction</u>
  Something cannot be both true and false at the same time and in the same way.
- <u>The Law of Excluded Middle</u>
  A statement is either true or false.

"Absolute truth exists in and of itself and is not based upon nor subject to man's opinion or intellectual validation." –mg

2. God's Word is verifiably, the preserved, authoritative, immutable, inerrant, infallible, everlasting and absolute TRUTH.

- **2 Timothy 3:16:** All scripture is given by inspiration of God, and is profitable for doctrine, for reproof, for correction, for instruction in righteousness.
- **Matthew 24:35:** Heaven and earth shall pass away, but my words shall not pass away.
- **2 Peter 1:16:** For we have not followed cunningly devised fables, when we made known unto you the power and coming of our Lord Jesus Christ, but were eyewitnesses of his majesty.

"Truth is not subjective, truth is objective, and that is irrefutable." -mg

Critical Thinking

The Bible, composed of 66 books of the Old and New Testament is the only infallible, plenary word of God, verbally and fully inspired; without error in the original autographs.

It is the supreme authority and final rule in all matters of faith and conduct; further, in all matters of our existence to which it speaks. The very revelation of God and His will, complete and sufficient in precept and principal, teaching God's plan of salvation for mankind. The final guide to interpretation of Scripture is Scripture itself.

Apart from a solid foundation of Absolute Truth, it is extremely difficult to hold fast your position of faith in adverse circumstances. *When life is coming at you a hundred miles an hour*, you need to know what you believe, and why you believe it!

For example; the facts of how The Holy Spirit moved upon forty different writers from diverse cultural backgrounds and languages, over more than a fifteen-hundred-year period of time, to pen the words He inspired them to record; All without a single contradiction, inaccuracy, or inconsistency; Verified historically, hermeneutically, and prophetically.

Speaking of the integrity of the Bible, prophesies and scientific advances foretold in Scripture coming to pass in specific detail, is mind boggling. The mathematical odds for this to happen by chance are astronomical! But this consideration goes far beyond just some events. There are verifiably, hundreds upon hundreds of prophesies that happened just as they were foretold in the Scriptures, far in advance. *The entirety of God's Word so clearly reveals His direct immanent interaction with mankind.*

God meticulously and miraculously preserved His Word throughout history. The number of New Testament manuscripts known to archeologists and historians exceeds **20,000**. And quotations from the early Church Fathers (Christian leaders) are more than **86,000**. These numbers represent "cataloged" manuscripts and writings. There are untold numbers of documented findings that are not yet cataloged on record. Then of course many copies of ancient Hebrew Scriptures exist, including the Dead Sea Scrolls that contain every book of the Old Testament except Esther. Not to mention, the works of secular historians, in which observations and reports were recorded from their first-hand experience, that verify the Biblical accounts of history.

Now, here are some facts that bring things into perspective.

Of other notable literary works of historic value, notice the number of copies on record, compared to the 20,000+ copies of New Testament Bible manuscripts:

- Homer's Iliad ---- 643 copies
- Sophocles ---- 193 copies
- Aristotle ---- 49 copies
- Cesar (Gallic Wars) ---- 10 copies

The Word of God (The Holy Bible) is more than a literary work that came by natural means... More than a collection of excellent historical records, with stories and illustrations for our entertainment... The Bible is not a collage of disjointed diverse topics and perspectives. No, **The Bible is the unified history of God's plan of Redemption for mankind.** (*The instruction manual for life*).

Jesus, who is Christ, our Lord and Savior, is the express theme of every book of the Bible, from Genesis through Revelation. From the five-hundred-foot view (so to speak), the Christocentric theme flows throughout the entirety of God's Word. Supernaturally comprised of:

- 5 books of the Pentateuch (*Hebrew Tora*)
- 12 books of History
- 5 books of Poetry
- 5 Major Prophets
- 12 Minor Prophets
- 4 Gospels
- 1 book of History (*Post Calvary – Church Age*)
- 21 Letters (*Epistles*)
- 1 book of Prophesy (*Revelation*)

I want to encourage my audience to do a study, research and find out the history of how we came to have The Holy Bible, "God's Word." It will be an invaluable foundation of certainty, to know that The Bible is more than reliable; It is verifiably the actual Word of God to you.

"And ye shall know the truth, and the truth shall make you free."

John 8:32

Personal Note from the Author

It is with great joy and excitement, that I have the privilege to share these things with you. To think that this information may help you to understand what The Lord, Almighty God has given to you.

And upon your decision to receive His gift, you are about to be forever changed by a supernatural miracle of astounding eternal affects.

You see, the whole idea of this book & presentation, is to inform you.

Romans 10:14 reads: How then shall they call on him in whom they have not believed? and how shall they believe in him of whom they have not heard? and how shall they hear without a preacher?

Sharing this message of The Gospel with you is an assignment of a lifetime. It's something I cherish, as it has eternal value and implications. For this reason, I want to be careful to present an accurate and concise invitation to receive God's gift.

Romans 6:23 reads: For the wages of sin is death; but the gift of God is eternal life through Jesus Christ our Lord.

God's gift of Salvation is simply conditioned upon personal choice. An act of your will to believe and receive what Jesus did for you. As you make Jesus Lord of your life, the miracle of regeneration takes place. Your Spirit will be "Born Again" (A new creation). You will be "Saved," Redeemed, Justified, and MADE Righteous by Him. *Hallelujah!*

The New Testament Greek word for Salvation is Sozo; Soteria; Please be encouraged to study this term out for yourself. You will find that God's Salvation covers every aspect of our being—Spirit, Soul, and Body. "Everything we will ever need in our existence."

God's Perfect Love, Perfect Plans, and Perfect Provisions.

"I pray for you right now by the authority of Jesus Christ. For all who will receive it, this word transcends time and distance, to affect your life from this moment, and forever; Thank You Lord for Your Anointing that destroys every yoke of bondage, and every work of darkness. I send Your Word to open the eyes of this dear one's heart, to see and receive Your plans and purpose for them. Thank You Lord Jesus." Amen

(Stay in agreement with this prayer, by faith, always).

Be Blessed!

Understanding Life's Narrative

God of all creation is perfect Love. Perfect Love has a perfect plan and purpose for you. But it's up to you if you want it, or not!

Every person on the planet, past, present, and future, is in the same predicament. We are separated from God because the first man that God created made the ultimate bad choice!

The first man and woman, Adam and Eve, exercised their free will by choosing to violate God's ordinance. It was an act of high treason, which allowed *satan* to usurp the authority and dominion that God had appointed to mankind; Adam relinquished that position of dominion and right standing with God, thereby causing entropy in creation by the sin condition. Every person born since Adam has inherited "the sin condition." *(More explanation to follow).*

For this reason, God implemented "The plan of Salvation," whereby He came in the flesh, to reconcile us and legally purchase our pardon from the penalty of sin. This is God's plan of Salvation.

"For God so loved the world, that He gave His only begotten Son, that whosoever believeth in Him should not perish, but have everlasting life. For God sent not His son into the world to condemn the world; but that the world through Him might be saved" **John 3:16 & 17.**

God is perfect love. The Creator and giver of life, is Love personified. And Perfect Love has always had our best interest in mind. Created in the very image of God Himself, humankind is the very focus and objective purpose for all that the Lord God made. It is easy to observe and recognize the intricate detail of order, which governs all that exists; including time, the universe, and the complex systems of creation's infrastructure, all for our benefit. Our life and purpose designed by Perfect Love even comes with an instruction manual. The provisions that God made for us are defined in that manual, which is the Holy Bible, The Word of God.

Yes, Almighty God, The author and Creator of life, gave us an authoritative overview of His plans and purpose for His beloved creation. In one portion of His instruction manual, we find an interesting statement: *"Without faith it is impossible to please Him."*
Hebrews 11:6

Rhymes of Reason

Why does God want us to trust Him so much ? Why is our faith centered on His Word so necessary? Is it because He takes pleasure in our challenges? Is it because He created life to be some sort of obstacle course, by which He is entertained with our actions and reactions? Does God require us to walk by faith and to take Him at His word because He wants to see us jump through religious hoops? The answer to these questions is a resounding **NO!**

The reason that our faith and trust pleases God is because He wants what's best for us. In order for The Word of God, (which is the will of God), to be fulfilled in a person's life, that individual must choose to receive His Word, (His will).

Every plan and purpose, every desire and thought that God has for us, is for our good. The Bible reveals God's character. Yet, there are people who spread malign misinformation and lies, either by ignorance or by the influence of satan, the illegitimate little god of this world.

Such as the claims that God is responsible for everything that happens in the world, both good and bad. This is absurd! It's satan that perpetrates all the evil in this world.

It is impossible for God to be an accomplice to anything that violates His will. He cannot contradict His Word.

God's plans are good and Holy and perfect, because God is Holy. Howbeit, our cooperation is essential to actuate those plans, allowing them to be fulfilled. God created humankind to have autonomy in acts of our will as free moral agents. Each individual person has the freedom of choice in all that they do, say, think or believe. However, with that freedom of choice there also comes responsibility, accountability and ultimately the results that our choices and actions produce. It is simply a fundamental law and principle of order that governs all of creation. Every seed produces after it's own kind. "We reap what we sow" **(See Galatians 6:7-8)**.

Let's look at some Scripture, (God's instruction manual), in which we can see the importance of our choices and how Perfect Love is God's motive for asking us to receive His plan.

> **Deuteronomy 30:19** I call heaven and earth to record this day against you, that I have set before you life and death,

blessing and cursing. Therefore choose life, that both thou and thy seed may live.

Romans 6:23 For the wages of sin is death; but the gift of God is eternal life through Jesus Christ our Lord.

Romans 10:8-10 (MEV) This is the word of faith that we preach: that if you confess with your mouth Jesus is Lord, and believe in your heart that God has raised Him from the dead, you will be saved; for with the heart one believes unto righteousness, and with the mouth confession is made unto salvation.

Ephesians 2:8-9 For by grace are ye saved through faith; and that not of yourselves: it is the gift of God: Not of works, lest any man should boast.

Romans 3:22-24 (MEV) This righteousness of God comes through faith in Jesus Christ to all and upon all who believe, for there is no distinction. For all have sinned and come short of the glory of God, being justified freely by His grace through the redemption that is in Christ Jesus.

Proverbs 4:20-22 (NKJV) My son, give attention to my words; Incline your ear to my sayings. Do not let them depart from your eyes; Keep them in the midst of your heart; For they are life to those who find them, And health to all their flesh.

What are the most important things we must understand from this narrative and analysis of our existence?

- Perfect Love has perfect plans & desires for us.
- Perfect Love does not force us to receive Him.
- Trust and faith in God is a matter of personal choice.
- Desired results require specific actions.
- Destiny is by choice not by chance.

This is why God compels us to act in faith toward Him.

All of creation is governed by the order that God designed and established from the beginning, including humankind's free moral agency, (freedom of choice).

The purpose and intent of this book is not to delve into systematic theology in attempt to support dogmas or denominational perspectives. The purpose and intent of this book is to bring attention to the essential mandates of God's Word regarding His Sovereign and perfect Will for mankind.

God did not create humankind as robots programmed without prerogative of choice. The first created man and woman exercised their freedom of choice in a direction that separated them from a right relationship with God. Thereby, the effects of that original sin have been the inheritance of all humanity. Adam and Eve's choice brought on the prevailing sin condition in the world, evident by the evil influence of *satan, the illegitimate little god of this world*. Adam and Eve's choice allowed the devil to illegally usurp the authority and dominion that God designated for humankind. In a fallen state of irreversible depravity, humanity is incapable of saving itself. Therefore, God made provision of reconciliation, redemption and freedom from the consequences of sin. (If we so choose).

That provision is His "**gift**" of Salvation through Jesus Christ, for everyone who will believe and receive His gift.

This is why the apostle Paul said; *"I am not ashamed of the gospel of Christ, for it is the power of God unto salvation for everyone that believes."* **Romans 1:16 (NKJV).**

"Love cannot be fulfilled until it is received."

The definition of fulfilled includes: Accomplished; Completed; Plans carried out; To bring into actuality; Effect or make real; To do, perform, (a task or order); To meet a requirement or condition.

To understand this premise will forever shape your perception, as it applies to the entirety of God's covenant Word. A word study of the original Greek text reveals that God's *Soteria* (salvation), is inclusive of every aspect of our being, Spirit, Soul, and Body.

Need healing? Okay, The instruction manual describes how Jesus was wounded for our transgressions, bruised for our iniquities: the chastisement of our peace was upon Him; and with His stripes, we are healed. **Isaiah 53:5** (also see 1 Peter 2:24)

However, as with all of our Heavenly Father's provisions, desired results require specific actions.

Here are some bullet points to summarize this profound message that Perfect Love is presenting to you:

- God watches over His Word to perform it (not the opinions and ideologies of man).

- God's Word, *the Bible as we have it,* is His Will, revealing His plans, purpose, and provision.

- God's Word is the very essence of God Himself.

- Receiving Him is essential to cooperating with Him. *(Allowing His Word to be manifest in our life).*

- Believing Him is the prerequisite to receiving Him. *(Again, His Word is the essence of His Will and who He is).*

How can a person believe in what they have not yet heard?

> *"Faith comes by hearing, and hearing by The Word of God."* **Romans 10:17**

Destiny is either by deliberate choice or by default. *Default is effectively choosing something other than God's Will, by not actively making the choice at all.* Anything other than God's Will has it's origin in the sin condition of this world, caused by man's original choice to rebel against God, producing undesirable results.

Love must be received to be fulfilled. Make no mistake; destiny is by choice, not by chance.

> *"For the wages of sin is death; but the gift of God is eternal life through Jesus Christ our Lord."* **Romans 6:23**

Have you ever given this proposition any serious thought?

If today was your last day on this earth, do you know where you would spend eternity?

When do you think would be the best time to make an informed decision regarding your destiny?

Prayer to Receive Salvation

You can receive God's wonderful gift of Salvation right now. Simply ask Him. Your prayer would sound something like this:

> Father God, I come to You in the name of Jesus.
>
> You said in Your word that *"whosoever shall call upon the name of The Lord shall be saved."* **(Acts 2:21)**
>
> Father, I ask You now for Your gift of Salvation. I repent and receive Your forgiveness for all unrighteousness. Thank You for redeeming me from the penalty of sin. Thank You for justifying me, (just-as-if-I-had never sinned).
>
> I confess Jesus as my Savior and Lord of my Life according to **Romans 10:9-10**: *"If thou shalt confess with thy mouth The Lord Jesus, and shalt believe in thine heart that God hath raised Him from the dead, thou shalt be saved. For with the heart man believeth unto righteousness; and with the mouth confession is made unto Salvation."*
>
> Thank You Lord, according to Your word, I am now saved. I belong to you now. I will from now on, endeavor to cooperate with You, so that You can fulfill every plan and purpose you have for me. Thank You for helping me.

Please be encouraged; Spend time with the Lord and with people who love the Lord. *"Faith comes by hearing, and hearing by The Word of God."* **(see Romans 10:17)**. I would suggest to you that doubt and unbelief comes by hearing what the world has to say, influenced by the devil.

As in any relationship, what you put in is what you get out.

The instruction manual says: *"Submit yourselves therefore to God. Resist the devil, and he will flee from you. Draw nigh to God, and He will draw nigh to you"* **(James 4:7-8)**.

And remember, God says that He watches over His Word to perform it **Jeremiah 1:12**. (Not the opinions of man).

For the desired results of God's plans, our faith must be centered on the Word of God, not on the opinions and ideologies of man! Absolute truth exists in and of itself and is not based upon nor subject to man's opinion or intellectual validation.

God's Word must be the focus and foundation of our prayers. Please see **Isaiah 55:10-11** and grow from there. (His Word will not return to Him void.)

Congratulations, and God Bless you. - *MG*

Prayer to Receive the Baptism in The Holy Spirit

(Please see Poem on page 86)

Subsequent to receiving the gift of Salvation, as a child of God you may now be endued with the power to live a victorious Christian life. The Holy Spirit will enable you, equip you and help you to walk in the fullness of God's plans and purpose.

He is the Paraclete, our Dear Comforter.

Among the many places in God's Word that explain this wonderful attribute of Salvation, let's look at the following for at least a beginning edification:

Matthew 3:16 "I indeed baptize you with water unto repentance: but he that cometh after me is mightier than I, whose shoes I am not worthy to bear: He shall baptize you with The Holy Ghost, and with fire."

John 15:26 "But when The comforter is come, whom I will send unto you from The Father, even the Spirit of truth, which proceedeth from The Father, He shall testify of me."

Acts 2:4 "And they were all filled with The Holy Ghost, and began to speak with other tongues, as The Spirit gave them utterance.

Acts 2:38,39 "Then Peter said unto them, Repent, and be baptized every one of you in the name of Jesus Christ for the remission of sins, and ye shall receive the gift of The Holy Ghost.For the promise is unto you, and your children, and to all that are afar off, even as many as The Lord our God shall call."

Acts 19:2, 6 "He said unto them, Have ye received The Holy Ghost since ye believed ? And they said unto him,We have not so much as heard whether there be any Holy Ghost." And when Paul laid his hands upon them, the Holy Ghost came on them; and they spake with tongues, and prophesied."

Luke 11:13 "How much more shall your heavenly Father give the Holy Spirit to them that ask Him ?"

Upon receiving the gift of Salvation, you have been made the righteousness of God by Jesus Christ our Lord. **(See 2 Cor. 5:21)**

Now, receive the promised gift of the Holy Spirit. Simply ask Father God to fill you with His Holy Spirit. Be sensitive to His voice as He speaks into your heart.

Please be mindful that often the Lord will speak in a still, small voice on the inside of you. If you are busy and the cares of this world are cluttering your heart, perhaps you think God will be okay with competing for your affection. Well, you may miss hearing Him speak.

As you seek to draw near to the Lord in all honesty and sincerity, He will draw near to you and fulfill your heart's desire to be baptized in His Spirit. It is that simple. **Your hunger is the key factor.**

Ask the Lord to sanctify you, "set you apart for His purpose." Continue to press in. Give Jesus the place of preeminence.

> "For all the promises of God in Him are yea, and in Him Amen, unto the glory of God by us." **2 Corinthians 1:20**

The Word of God is the very essence of God Himself.

The Word of God is the Will of God, forever settled.

Faith centered on the known will of God produces desired results.

Accept nothing less, nothing more, and nothing else.

May we encourage you to fellowship with people who are also passionate in their pursuit of knowing God. The primary way God reveals Himself and His perfect Love is with His Word, The Bible.

Congratulations and God bless.

Michael Gittens, Evangelist & Fellow Servant

Notes

Notes

Notes

About the Author

I'm always interested to know a little bit about the person who is trying to persuade me, or inform me.
After all, information shapes our worldview and perception.
It's important to verify the source, right? So, I will share a few things about myself that will at least give my audience some insight.

Most people call me Mike.
My wife and I live in beautiful North Georgia.
(She deserves some sort of award or a medal for putting up with me for nearly four decades now. See my dedication page for more about her.) I am blessed with all that's important to me, and family is at the top of that list.
Our career has primarily been in the construction industry.
"Custom homes and renovations is what I do...
A fellow servant in the furtherance of the Gospel is what I am."

Formally set forth and ordained in 2006.
A non-denominational, Evangelical Minister;
Theologically and experientially Pentecostal;
Adherent to the inerrancy of canonical Scripture and all essential doctrines set forth therein.

My highest honor and greatest privilege is to participate in things of eternal value.

In summary, the following bullet points touch on some relevant interests and accolades that further represent who I am:

- Patriot, Constitutionist.
- Military service: United States Marine Corps.
  "Semper Fidelis."
- Certified Master Chaplain, Emergency Services, Fire & Police, and Jail & Prison Ministry.
- Biblical Counselor
- **Jesus is Lord. He is preeminent in my life and aspirations.**

Thank you for the opportunity to introduce myself and to share the contents of this book. I've had no formal training in writing poetry, this is just something that began coming into my heart one day...

I thank the Lord for this assignment.

Please find our contact information and a brief overview of Michael Gittens Ministries on the following page.

Postscript

Thank you for the opportunity
to share these things of eternal value...
All glory and honor and praise be to The Lord, Almighty God.
May His plans and purpose be fulfilled in all we do.

Mission Statement:
 "To prove what is that good and acceptable
 and perfect will of God." **(Rom. 12:2)**
Vision:
Delivering The Gospel of Jesus Christ in practical application
and demonstration of the written Word of God.
Objectives:
* Clear, effective presentation of God's plan of salvation,
 revealing His love to all people, initiating their response.
* Networking within the Body of Christ to promote
 corporate and individual consecration, effecting revival.

• Michael Gittens Ministries •

www.michaelgittensministries.com

www.ingramcontent.com/pod-product-compliance
Lightning Source LLC
Chambersburg PA
CBHW071451080526
44587CB00014B/2063